ATS-150   ADMISSION TEST SERIES

This is your
PASSBOOK for...

Certified Dental Assistant (CDA)

Test Preparation Study Guide
Questions & Answers

COPYRIGHT NOTICE

This book is SOLELY intended for, is sold ONLY to, and its use is RESTRICTED to individual, bona fide applicants or candidates who qualify by virtue of having seriously filed applications for appropriate license, certificate, professional and/or promotional advancement, higher school matriculation, scholarship, or other legitimate requirements of education and/or governmental authorities.

This book is NOT intended for use, class instruction, tutoring, training, duplication, copying, reprinting, excerption, or adaptation, etc., by:

1) Other publishers
2) Proprietors and/or Instructors of "Coaching" and/or Preparatory Courses
3) Personnel and/or Training Divisions of commercial, industrial, and governmental organizations
4) Schools, colleges, or universities and/or their departments and staffs, including teachers and other personnel
5) Testing Agencies or Bureaus
6) Study groups which seek by the purchase of a single volume to copy and/or duplicate and/or adapt this material for use by the group as a whole without having purchased individual volumes for each of the members of the group
7) Et al.

Such persons would be in violation of appropriate Federal and State statutes.

PROVISION OF LICENSING AGREEMENTS – Recognized educational, commercial, industrial, and governmental institutions and organizations, and others legitimately engaged in educational pursuits, including training, testing, and measurement activities, may address request for a licensing agreement to the copyright owners, who will determine whether, and under what conditions, including fees and charges, the materials in this book may be used them. In other words, a licensing facility exists for the legitimate use of the material in this book on other than an individual basis. However, it is asseverated and affirmed here that the material in this book CANNOT be used without the receipt of the express permission of such a licensing agreement from the Publishers. Inquiries re licensing should be addressed to the company, attention rights and permissions department.

All rights reserved, including the right of reproduction in whole or in part, in any form or by any means, electronic or mechanical, including photocopying, recording, or by any information storage and retrieval system, without permission in writing from the Publisher.

Copyright © 2024 by
National Learning Corporation

212 Michael Drive, Syosset, NY 11791
(516) 921-8888 • www.passbooks.com
E-mail: info@passbooks.com

PUBLISHED IN THE UNITED STATES OF AMERICA

PASSBOOK® SERIES

THE *PASSBOOK® SERIES* has been created to prepare applicants and candidates for the ultimate academic battlefield – the examination room.

At some time in our lives, each and every one of us may be required to take an examination – for validation, matriculation, admission, qualification, registration, certification, or licensure.

Based on the assumption that every applicant or candidate has met the basic formal educational standards, has taken the required number of courses, and read the necessary texts, the *PASSBOOK® SERIES* furnishes the one special preparation which may assure passing with confidence, instead of failing with insecurity. Examination questions – together with answers – are furnished as the basic vehicle for study so that the mysteries of the examination and its compounding difficulties may be eliminated or diminished by a sure method.

This book is meant to help you pass your examination provided that you qualify and are serious in your objective.

The entire field is reviewed through the huge store of content information which is succinctly presented through a provocative and challenging approach – the question-and-answer method.

A climate of success is established by furnishing the correct answers at the end of each test.

You soon learn to recognize types of questions, forms of questions, and patterns of questioning. You may even begin to anticipate expected outcomes.

You perceive that many questions are repeated or adapted so that you can gain acute insights, which may enable you to score many sure points.

You learn how to confront new questions, or types of questions, and to attack them confidently and work out the correct answers.

You note objectives and emphases, and recognize pitfalls and dangers, so that you may make positive educational adjustments.

Moreover, you are kept fully informed in relation to new concepts, methods, practices, and directions in the field.

You discover that you are actually taking the examination all the time: you are preparing for the examination by "taking" an examination, not by reading extraneous and/or supererogatory textbooks.

In short, this PASSBOOK®, used directedly, should be an important factor in helping you to pass your test.

Certified Dental Assistant (CDA) Exam

The CDA exam consists of 320 multiple-choice items. You will have 4 hours to take the exam.

CDA Exam Contents

The CDA exam is made up of three components. The candidate must meet minimum performance standards in each component to earn a CDA Certification. These components are:

General Chairside (GC)

120 multiple-choice items-1½ hours testing time

Topics	% on exam
Collection and recording of clinical data	10
Chairside dental procedures	45
Chairside dental materials (preparation, manipulation, application)	11
Lab materials and procedures	4
Patient education and oral health management	10
Prevention & management of emergencies	14
Office management procedures	6

Radiation Health & Safety (RHS)

100 multiple-choice items-1½ hours testing time

Topics	% on exam
Expose and evaluate (intraoral, extraoral)	37
Process	16
Mount/label	11
Radiation safety-patient	24
Radiation safety-operator	12

Infection Control (ICE)

100 multiple-choice items-1½ hours testing time

Topics	% on exam
Patient and dental health care worker education	10
Prevent cross-contamination & transmission	20
Maintain aseptic conditions	10
Perform sterilization procedures	15
Environmental asepsis	15
Occupational safety	30

HOW TO TAKE A TEST

You have studied long, hard and conscientiously.

With your official admission card in hand, and your heart pounding, you have been admitted to the examination room.

You note that there are several hundred other applicants in the examination room waiting to take the same test.

They all appear to be equally well prepared.

You know that nothing but your best effort will suffice. The "moment of truth" is at hand: you now have to demonstrate objectively, in writing, your knowledge of content and your understanding of subject matter.

You are fighting the most important battle of your life—to pass and/or score high on an examination which will determine your career and provide the economic basis for your livelihood.

What extra, special things should you know and should you do in taking the examination?

I. YOU MUST PASS AN EXAMINATION

A. WHAT EVERY CANDIDATE SHOULD KNOW
Examination applicants often ask us for help in preparing for the written test. What can I study in advance? What kinds of questions will be asked? How will the test be given? How will the papers be graded?

B. HOW ARE EXAMS DEVELOPED?
Examinations are carefully written by trained technicians who are specialists in the field known as "psychological measurement," in consultation with recognized authorities in the field of work that the test will cover. These experts recommend the subject matter areas or skills to be tested; only those knowledges or skills important to your success on the job are included. The most reliable books and source materials available are used as references. Together, the experts and technicians judge the difficulty level of the questions.
Test technicians know how to phrase questions so that the problem is clearly stated. Their ethics do not permit "trick" or "catch" questions. Questions may have been tried out on sample groups, or subjected to statistical analysis, to determine their usefulness.
Written tests are often used in combination with performance tests, ratings of training and experience, and oral interviews. All of these measures combine to form the best-known means of finding the right person for the right job.

II. HOW TO PASS THE WRITTEN TEST

A. BASIC STEPS

1) Study the announcement

How, then, can you know what subjects to study? Our best answer is: "Learn as much as possible about the class of positions for which you've applied." The exam will test the knowledge, skills and abilities needed to do the work.

Your most valuable source of information about the position you want is the official exam announcement. This announcement lists the training and experience qualifications. Check these standards and apply only if you come reasonably close to meeting them. Many jurisdictions preview the written test in the exam announcement by including a section called "Knowledge and Abilities Required," "Scope of the Examination," or some similar heading. Here you will find out specifically what fields will be tested.

2) Choose appropriate study materials

If the position for which you are applying is technical or advanced, you will read more advanced, specialized material. If you are already familiar with the basic principles of your field, elementary textbooks would waste your time. Concentrate on advanced textbooks and technical periodicals. Think through the concepts and review difficult problems in your field.

These are all general sources. You can get more ideas on your own initiative, following these leads. For example, training manuals and publications of the government agency which employs workers in your field can be useful, particularly for technical and professional positions. A letter or visit to the government department involved may result in more specific study suggestions, and certainly will provide you with a more definite idea of the exact nature of the position you are seeking.

3) Study this book!

III. KINDS OF TESTS

Tests are used for purposes other than measuring knowledge and ability to perform specified duties. For some positions, it is equally important to test ability to make adjustments to new situations or to profit from training. In others, basic mental abilities not dependent on information are essential. Questions which test these things may not appear as pertinent to the duties of the position as those which test for knowledge and information. Yet they are often highly important parts of a fair examination. For very general questions, it is almost impossible to help you direct your study efforts. What we can do is to point out some of the more common of these general abilities needed in public service positions and describe some typical questions.

1) General information

Broad, general information has been found useful for predicting job success in some kinds of work. This is tested in a variety of ways, from vocabulary lists to questions about current events. Basic background in some field of work, such as sociology or economics, may be sampled in a group of questions. Often these are principles which have become familiar to most persons through exposure rather than through formal training. It is difficult to advise you how to study for these questions; being alert to the world around you is our best suggestion.

2) Verbal ability
An example of an ability needed in many positions is verbal or language ability. Verbal ability is, in brief, the ability to use and understand words. Vocabulary and grammar tests are typical measures of this ability. Reading comprehension or paragraph interpretation questions are common in many kinds of civil service tests. You are given a paragraph of written material and asked to find its central meaning.

IV. KINDS OF QUESTIONS

1. Multiple-choice Questions
Most popular of the short-answer questions is the "multiple choice" or "best answer" question. It can be used, for example, to test for factual knowledge, ability to solve problems or judgment in meeting situations found at work.
A multiple-choice question is normally one of three types:
- It can begin with an incomplete statement followed by several possible endings. You are to find the one ending which best completes the statement, although some of the others may not be entirely wrong.
- It can also be a complete statement in the form of a question which is answered by choosing one of the statements listed.
- It can be in the form of a problem – again you select the best answer.

Here is an example of a multiple-choice question with a discussion which should give you some clues as to the method for choosing the right answer:

When an employee has a complaint about his assignment, the action which will best help him overcome his difficulty is to
    A. discuss his difficulty with his coworkers
    B. take the problem to the head of the organization
    C. take the problem to the person who gave him the assignment
    D. say nothing to anyone about his complaint

In answering this question, you should study each of the choices to find which is best. Consider choice "A" – Certainly an employee may discuss his complaint with fellow employees, but no change or improvement can result, and the complaint remains unresolved. Choice "B" is a poor choice since the head of the organization probably does not know what assignment you have been given, and taking your problem to him is known as "going over the head" of the supervisor. The supervisor, or person who made the assignment, is the person who can clarify it or correct any injustice. Choice "C" is, therefore, correct. To say nothing, as in choice "D," is unwise. Supervisors have and interest in knowing the problems employees are facing, and the employee is seeking a solution to his problem.

2. True/False

3. Matching Questions
Matching an answer from a column of choices within another column.

V. RECORDING YOUR ANSWERS

Computer terminals are used more and more today for many different kinds of exams.

For an examination with very few applicants, you may be told to record your answers in the test booklet itself. Separate answer sheets are much more common. If this separate answer sheet is to be scored by machine – and this is often the case – it is highly important that you mark your answers correctly in order to get credit.

VI. BEFORE THE TEST

YOUR PHYSICAL CONDITION IS IMPORTANT

If you are not well, you can't do your best work on tests. If you are half asleep, you can't do your best either. Here are some tips:

1) Get about the same amount of sleep you usually get. Don't stay up all night before the test, either partying or worrying—DON'T DO IT!
2) If you wear glasses, be sure to wear them when you go to take the test. This goes for hearing aids, too.
3) If you have any physical problems that may keep you from doing your best, be sure to tell the person giving the test. If you are sick or in poor health, you relay cannot do your best on any test. You can always come back and take the test some other time.

Common sense will help you find procedures to follow to get ready for an examination. Too many of us, however, overlook these sensible measures. Indeed, nervousness and fatigue have been found to be the most serious reasons why applicants fail to do their best on civil service tests. Here is a list of reminders:

- Begin your preparation early – Don't wait until the last minute to go scurrying around for books and materials or to find out what the position is all about.
- Prepare continuously – An hour a night for a week is better than an all-night cram session. This has been definitely established. What is more, a night a week for a month will return better dividends than crowding your study into a shorter period of time.
- Locate the place of the exam – You have been sent a notice telling you when and where to report for the examination. If the location is in a different town or otherwise unfamiliar to you, it would be well to inquire the best route and learn something about the building.
- Relax the night before the test – Allow your mind to rest. Do not study at all that night. Plan some mild recreation or diversion; then go to bed early and get a good night's sleep.
- Get up early enough to make a leisurely trip to the place for the test – This way unforeseen events, traffic snarls, unfamiliar buildings, etc. will not upset you.
- Dress comfortably – A written test is not a fashion show. You will be known by number and not by name, so wear something comfortable.
- Leave excess paraphernalia at home – Shopping bags and odd bundles will get in your way. You need bring only the items mentioned in the official notice you received; usually everything you need is provided. Do not bring reference books to the exam. They will only confuse those last minutes and be taken away from you when in the test room.

- Arrive somewhat ahead of time – If because of transportation schedules you must get there very early, bring a newspaper or magazine to take your mind off yourself while waiting.
- Locate the examination room – When you have found the proper room, you will be directed to the seat or part of the room where you will sit. Sometimes you are given a sheet of instructions to read while you are waiting. Do not fill out any forms until you are told to do so; just read them and be prepared.
- Relax and prepare to listen to the instructions
- If you have any physical problem that may keep you from doing your best, be sure to tell the test administrator. If you are sick or in poor health, you really cannot do your best on the exam. You can come back and take the test some other time.

VII. AT THE TEST

The day of the test is here and you have the test booklet in your hand. The temptation to get going is very strong. Caution! There is more to success than knowing the right answers. You must know how to identify your papers and understand variations in the type of short-answer question used in this particular examination. Follow these suggestions for maximum results from your efforts:

1) Cooperate with the monitor

The test administrator has a duty to create a situation in which you can be as much at ease as possible. He will give instructions, tell you when to begin, check to see that you are marking your answer sheet correctly, and so on. He is not there to guard you, although he will see that your competitors do not take unfair advantage. He wants to help you do your best.

2) Listen to all instructions

Don't jump the gun! Wait until you understand all directions. In most civil service tests you get more time than you need to answer the questions. So don't be in a hurry. Read each word of instructions until you clearly understand the meaning. Study the examples, listen to all announcements and follow directions. Ask questions if you do not understand what to do.

3) Identify your papers

Civil service exams are usually identified by number only. You will be assigned a number; you must not put your name on your test papers. Be sure to copy your number correctly. Since more than one exam may be given, copy your exact examination title.

4) Plan your time

Unless you are told that a test is a "speed" or "rate of work" test, speed itself is usually not important. Time enough to answer all the questions will be provided, but this does not mean that you have all day. An overall time limit has been set. Divide the total time (in minutes) by the number of questions to determine the approximate time you have for each question.

5) Do not linger over difficult questions

If you come across a difficult question, mark it with a paper clip (useful to have along) and come back to it when you have been through the booklet. One caution if you do this – be sure to skip a number on your answer sheet as well. Check often to be sure that you have not lost your place and that you are marking in the row numbered the same as the question you are answering.

6) Read the questions

Be sure you know what the question asks! Many capable people are unsuccessful because they failed to read the questions correctly.

7) Answer all questions

Unless you have been instructed that a penalty will be deducted for incorrect answers, it is better to guess than to omit a question.

8) Speed tests

It is often better NOT to guess on speed tests. It has been found that on timed tests people are tempted to spend the last few seconds before time is called in marking answers at random – without even reading them – in the hope of picking up a few extra points. To discourage this practice, the instructions may warn you that your score will be "corrected" for guessing. That is, a penalty will be applied. The incorrect answers will be deducted from the correct ones, or some other penalty formula will be used.

9) Review your answers

If you finish before time is called, go back to the questions you guessed or omitted to give them further thought. Review other answers if you have time.

10) Return your test materials

If you are ready to leave before others have finished or time is called, take ALL your materials to the monitor and leave quietly. Never take any test material with you. The monitor can discover whose papers are not complete, and taking a test booklet may be grounds for disqualification.

VIII. EXAMINATION TECHNIQUES

1) Read the general instructions carefully. These are usually printed on the first page of the exam booklet. As a rule, these instructions refer to the timing of the examination; the fact that you should not start work until the signal and must stop work at a signal, etc. If there are any special instructions, such as a choice of questions to be answered, make sure that you note this instruction carefully.

2) When you are ready to start work on the examination, that is as soon as the signal has been given, read the instructions to each question booklet, underline any key words or phrases, such as least, best, outline, describe and the like. In this way you will tend to answer as requested rather than discover on reviewing your paper that you listed without describing, that you selected the worst choice rather than the best choice, etc.

3) If the examination is of the objective or multiple-choice type – that is, each question will also give a series of possible answers: A, B, C or D, and you are called upon to select the best answer and write the letter next to that answer on your answer paper – it is advisable to start answering each question in turn. There may be anywhere from 50 to 100 such questions in the three or four hours allotted and you can see how much time would be taken if you read through all the questions before beginning to answer any. Furthermore, if you

come across a question or group of questions which you know would be difficult to answer, it would undoubtedly affect your handling of all the other questions.

4) If the examination is of the essay type and contains but a few questions, it is a moot point as to whether you should read all the questions before starting to answer any one. Of course, if you are given a choice – say five out of seven and the like – then it is essential to read all the questions so you can eliminate the two that are most difficult. If, however, you are asked to answer all the questions, there may be danger in trying to answer the easiest one first because you may find that you will spend too much time on it. The best technique is to answer the first question, then proceed to the second, etc.

5) Time your answers. Before the exam begins, write down the time it started, then add the time allowed for the examination and write down the time it must be completed, then divide the time available somewhat as follows:
   - If 3-1/2 hours are allowed, that would be 210 minutes. If you have 80 objective-type questions, that would be an average of 2-1/2 minutes per question. Allow yourself no more than 2 minutes per question, or a total of 160 minutes, which will permit about 50 minutes to review.
   - If for the time allotment of 210 minutes there are 7 essay questions to answer, that would average about 30 minutes a question. Give yourself only 25 minutes per question so that you have about 35 minutes to review.

6) The most important instruction is to read each question and make sure you know what is wanted. The second most important instruction is to time yourself properly so that you answer every question. The third most important instruction is to answer every question. Guess if you have to but include something for each question. Remember that you will receive no credit for a blank and will probably receive some credit if you write something in answer to an essay question. If you guess a letter – say "B" for a multiple-choice question – you may have guessed right. If you leave a blank as an answer to a multiple-choice question, the examiners may respect your feelings but it will not add a point to your score. Some exams may penalize you for wrong answers, so in such cases only, you may not want to guess unless you have some basis for your answer.

7) Suggestions
   a. Objective-type questions
      1. Examine the question booklet for proper sequence of pages and questions
      2. Read all instructions carefully
      3. Skip any question which seems too difficult; return to it after all other questions have been answered
      4. Apportion your time properly; do not spend too much time on any single question or group of questions
      5. Note and underline key words – all, most, fewest, least, best, worst, same, opposite, etc.
      6. Pay particular attention to negatives
      7. Note unusual option, e.g., unduly long, short, complex, different or similar in content to the body of the question
      8. Observe the use of "hedging" words – probably, may, most likely, etc.

9. Make sure that your answer is put next to the same number as the question
10. Do not second-guess unless you have good reason to believe the second answer is definitely more correct
11. Cross out original answer if you decide another answer is more accurate; do not erase until you are ready to hand your paper in
12. Answer all questions; guess unless instructed otherwise
13. Leave time for review

b. Essay questions
   1. Read each question carefully
   2. Determine exactly what is wanted. Underline key words or phrases.
   3. Decide on outline or paragraph answer
   4. Include many different points and elements unless asked to develop any one or two points or elements
   5. Show impartiality by giving pros and cons unless directed to select one side only
   6. Make and write down any assumptions you find necessary to answer the questions
   7. Watch your English, grammar, punctuation and choice of words
   8. Time your answers; don't crowd material

8) Answering the essay question

Most essay questions can be answered by framing the specific response around several key words or ideas. Here are a few such key words or ideas:

M's: manpower, materials, methods, money, management
P's: purpose, program, policy, plan, procedure, practice, problems, pitfalls, personnel, public relations

a. Six basic steps in handling problems:
   1. Preliminary plan and background development
   2. Collect information, data and facts
   3. Analyze and interpret information, data and facts
   4. Analyze and develop solutions as well as make recommendations
   5. Prepare report and sell recommendations
   6. Install recommendations and follow up effectiveness

b. Pitfalls to avoid
   1. Taking things for granted – A statement of the situation does not necessarily imply that each of the elements is necessarily true; for example, a complaint may be invalid and biased so that all that can be taken for granted is that a complaint has been registered
   2. Considering only one side of a situation – Wherever possible, indicate several alternatives and then point out the reasons you selected the best one
   3. Failing to indicate follow up – Whenever your answer indicates action on your part, make certain that you will take proper follow-up action to see how successful your recommendations, procedures or actions turn out to be
   4. Taking too long in answering any single question – Remember to time your answers properly

EXAMINATION SECTION

EXAMINATION SECTION
TEST 1

DIRECTIONS: Each question or incomplete statement is followed by several suggested answers or completions. Select the one that BEST answers the question or completes the statement. *PRINT THE LETTER OF THE CORRECT ANSWER IN THE SPACE AT THE RIGHT.*

1. Which of the following medications would be contraindicated for a patient with severe hypertension? 1.____
    A. Fluoride
    B. Nitrous oxide
    C. Epinephrine
    D. Lidocaine

2. What type of anesthetic should be used if a patient is going to undergo a procedure that will last approximately 30 minutes? 2.____
    A. Mepivacaine with epinephrine
    B. Bupivacaine with epinephrine
    C. Prilocaine with epinephrine
    D. Lidocaine HCl

3. Which instrument comes in various types including straight, binangle, Wedelstaedt, and angle-former? 3.____
    A. Chisel   B. Hatchet   C. Excavator   D. Hoe

4. If you notice demineralization of the enamel on the lingual of anterior teeth, what is the underlying cause? 4.____
    A. Diabetes
    B. Hyperthyroidism
    C. Anorexia
    D. Bulimia

5. Which of the following is the surface of the tooth toward the midline? 5.____
    A. Mesial   B. Distal   C. Lingual   D. Buccal

6. Which of the following is the portion of the tooth that is covered with enamel? 6.____
    A. Anatomical   B. Proximal   C. Apical   D. Cervical

7. What is the depth of a normal sulcus? 7.____
    A. 1-2 mm   B. 2-3 mm   C. 3-4 mm   D. 4-5 mm

8. What impression material is used to take impressions for study models? 8.____
    A. Plaster   B. Alginate   C. Arginate   D. Calcitrate

9. What material is used to pour the impression for study models? 9.____
    A. Plaster
    B. Alginate
    C. Elastomers
    D. Zinc oxide eugenol

10. Which artery is used to monitor blood pressure in the dental office? 10.____
    A. Carotid   B. Brachial   C. Cephalic   D. Mesenteric

11. In an emergency situation, what artery is used to monitor pulse rate?
    A. Carotid B. Brachial C. Cephalic D. Mesenteric

12. If the patient is reclined at 45 degrees, on what quadrant would the dentist be working?
    A. 1 and 2 B. 2 and 3 C. 3 and 4 D. 1 and 4

13. At what clock position is the dental assistant seated for a right-handed dentist?
    A. 12 – 2 o'clock B. 2 – 4 o'clock C. 6 – 8 o'clock D. 8 – 10 o'clock

14. At what clock position is the dental assistant seated for a left-handed dentist?
    A. 12 – 2 o'clock B. 2 – 4 o'clock C. 6 – 8 o'clock D. 8 – 10 o'clock

15. What fingers are used to place instruments into the dentist's hand?
    A. Second finger, ring finger, and pinky
    B. Index finger, second finger, and ring finger
    C. Thumb, index finger, and pinky
    D. Thumb, index finger, and second finger

16. What fingers are used to retrieve dental instruments from the dentist?
    A. Thumb and index finger   B. Thumb and second finger
    C. Second finger and ring finger D. Ring finger and pinky

17. In which zone should the instrument tray be located?
    A. Static B. Assistant C. Transfer D. Operator

18. The area below the patient's nose where instruments are passed and received is referred to as the _____ zone.
    A. static B. assistant C. transfer D. operator

19. Which of the following is the CORRECT placement for the HVE tip?
    A. Superior to the tooth being worked on
    B. Inferior to the tooth being worked on
    C. One tooth distal to the tooth being worked on
    D. One tooth proximal to the tooth being worked on

20. Where should cotton rolls be placed when treating mandibular teeth?
    A. Mesially B. Distally C. Lingually D. Buccally

21. Where should cotton rolls be placed when treating maxillary teeth?
    A. Mesially B. Distally C. Lingually D. Buccally

22. A permanent dentition consists of how many teeth?
    A. 30 B. 32 C. 34 D. 36

23. Which teeth, shown in the image at the right, are commonly referred to as the "eye teeth"?
    A. Premolars
    B. Canines
    C. Incisors
    D. Bicuspids

24. A permanent dentition consists of how many premolars?
    A. 2   B. 4   C. 8   D. 12

25. Using the Universal System of tooth designation, what is tooth #22?
    A. Upper left central incisor
    B. Upper right lateral incisor
    C. Lower left canine
    D. Lower right canine

26. Using the International Standards Organization system of tooth recording, what is tooth #25?
    A. Lower left central incisor
    B. Lower right central incisor
    C. Upper left second premolar
    D. Upper right second premolar

27. Using Black's classification of cavities, a pit lesion on the buccal of molars and premolars is considered a class _____ restoration or cavity.
    A. I   B. II   C. III   D. IV

28. Which of the following refers to any tooth that remains unerupted in the jaw beyond the time at which it should normally erupt?
    A. Fused   B. Abraded   C. Impacted   D. Cemented

29. The high-speed contra-angle handpiece reaches a speed of _____ rpm.
    A. 150,000   B. 250,000   C. 350,000   D. 450,000

30. In the United States, nitrous oxide gas lines are what color?
    A. Red   B. Blue   C. Green   D. Black

KEY (CORRECT ANSWERS)

1.	C	11.	A	21.	D
2.	D	12.	C	22.	B
3.	A	13.	B	23.	B
4.	D	14.	D	24.	C
5.	A	15.	D	25.	C
6.	A	16.	D	26.	C
7.	B	17.	A	27.	A
8.	B	18.	C	28.	C
9.	A	19.	C	29.	D
10.	B	20.	C	30.	B

TEST 2

DIRECTIONS: Each question or incomplete statement is followed by several suggested answers or completions. Select the one that BEST answers the question or completes the statement. *PRINT THE LETTER OF THE CORRECT ANSWER IN THE SPACE AT THE RIGHT.*

1. Which of the following is a condition which will result if an alginate impression absorbs additional water by being stored in water or in a very wet paper towel? 1.____
   A. Imbibition   B. Hydrolysis
   C. Polymerization   D. Dessication

2. Which of the following waxes can be applied to the edge of the alginate trays to improve the fit of the tray? 2.____
   A. Utility   B. Inlay   C. Casting   D. Baseplate

3. Which of the following is defined as moving the tooth back and forth within the socket? 3.____
   A. Pronation   B. Supination   C. Luxation   D. Capitation

4. What type of forceps is designed to grasp the bifurcation of the root of a mandibular molar? 4.____
   A. Curved   B. Bayonet   C. Cowhorn   D. Universal

5. Which instrument would be used to measure the depth of the gingival sulcus? 5.____
   A. Cowhorn explorer   B. Shepherd's hook
   C. Periodontal explorer   D. Right angle explorer

6. Which instrument, shown in the image at the right, has a sharp round angular tip used to detect tooth anomalies? 6.____
   A. Cowhorn explorer
   B. Shepherd's hook
   C. Periodontal explorer
   D. Right angle explorer

7. Which instrument is commonly used to scale surfaces in the anterior region of the mouth? 7.____
   A. Curet scaler   B. Gracey scaler
   C. Straight sickle scaler   D. Modified sickle scaler

8. Which instrument, shown in the image at the right, is used to scale deep periodontal pockets or furcation areas?
   A. Curet scaler
   B. Gracey scaler
   C. Straight sickle scaler
   D. Modified sickle scaler

8.____

9. Where should the HVE tip be positioned when the operator is working on the labial of tooth #9?
   A. In the vestibule
   B. I the retromolar area
   C. On the opposite side of the tooth being prepared
   D. On the labial surface of the tooth being prepared

9.____

10. If a right-handed dentist is doing preparation on #30 MO, the dental assistant should place the HVE tip on the
    A. buccal of #30   B. buccal of #19
    C. lingual of #30   D. lingual of #19

10.____

11. The cement that has a sedative effect on the pulp is known as
    A. glass ionomer   B. zinc phosphate
    C. zinc oxide eugenol   D. zinc silicon phosphate

11.____

12. Which of the following techniques would be useful for caries removal?
    A. No. ¼ FG and explorer
    B. No. ¼ FG and spoon excavator
    C. No. 2 RA bur and spoon excavator
    D. No. 2 RA bur and enamel hatchet

12.____

13. Which part of the anesthetic syringe is different among the aspirating and non-aspirating varieties?
    A. Piston   B. Harpoon
    C. Syringe barrel   D. Metal thumb ring

13.____

14. For what purpose would a tooth be acid etched when using a composite restorative?
    A. To prepare the pulp
    B. To seal the dentinal tubules
    C. To form tags on the etched tooth surface
    D. To form a bond on the cavity structure of the tooth

14.____

15. Which of the following is an indication for pit and fissure sealants?
    A. Teeth are prone to caries.
    B. Teeth are not prone to caries.
    C. Teeth have sealants already present.
    D. The fossae are wide and easy to clean.

15.____

16. If a tooth has been avulsed, the tooth has been
    A. fractured
    B. sealed with a sealant
    C. restored with amalgam
    D. knocked free from the oral cavity

17. Which of the following is the MOST common type of attachment for fixed orthodontic appliances?
    A. Separator
    B. Arch wire
    C. Bonded bracket
    D. Orthodontic band

18. Which of the following is a thermoplastic material used to stabilize an anterior clamp?
    A. Floss
    B. Dri-angle
    C. Sticky wax
    D. Dental compound

19. What type of cement must be mixed on a glass slab?
    A. Calcium hydroxide
    B. Zinc phosphate
    C. Zinc oxide eugenol
    D. Zinc polycarbonate

20. What material is recommended for polishing filled hybrid composites and resin restorations?
    A. Tin oxide paste
    B. Aluminum oxide paste
    C. Diamond polishing paste
    D. Coarse polishing paste

21. Composite restorative materials are usually cured for what period of time with a halogen curing light?
    A. 3 seconds   B. 20 seconds   C. 60 seconds   D. 120 seconds

22. What instrument is used when ligating an archwire?
    A. Hemostats
    B. Howe pliers
    C. Utility pliers
    D. Ligature tying pliers

23. A periodontal probe is an example of what type of instrument?
    A. Accessory   B. Restorative   C. Examination   D. Hand cutting

24. Which of the following statements is TRUE regarding the angle of the bevel of the HVE tip?
    It should be
    A. parallel to the occlusal surface
    B. perpendicular to the occlusal surface
    C. parallel to the buccal and lingual surfaces
    D. perpendicular to the buccal and lingual surfaces

25. The tip of the composite curing light should be held at an angle of _____ degrees to the tooth.
    A. 10   B. 30   C. 45   D. 60

26. Which of the following is defined as a negative impression of the patient's dental arch?
    A. Die   B. Model   C. Cast   D. Impression

27. Which of the following refers to the process by which the resin material is changed from a pliable state to a hardened restoration?
    A. Microcuring
    B. Macrocuring
    C. Light curing
    D. Endothermic curing

27._____

28. Which of the following are the only nutrients that can build and repair body tissues?
    A. Proteins   B. Vitamins   C. Minerals   D. Carbohydrates

28._____

29. If a patient is prescribed to take a medication once every other day, what is the APPROPRIATE abbreviation for this prescription?
    A. q.d.   B. q.i.d.   C. q.o.d.   D. t.i.d.

29._____

30. Inflammation of the supporting tissues of the teeth that begins with gingivitis can progress into the connective tissue and alveolar bone that supports the teeth and become which of the following?
    A. Glossitis   B. Gangrene   C. Periodontitis   D. Epiglottitis

30._____

KEY (CORRECT ANSWERS)

1.	A	11.	C	21.	B
2.	A	12.	C	22.	D
3.	C	13.	B	23.	A
4.	C	14.	C	24.	C
5.	C	15.	A	25.	A
6.	A	16.	D	26.	D
7.	C	17.	C	27.	C
8.	B	18.	D	28.	A
9.	C	19.	B	29.	C
10.	C	20.	B	30.	C

TEST 3

DIRECTIONS: Each question or incomplete statement is followed by several suggested answers or completions. Select the one that BEST answers the question or completes the statement. *PRINT THE LETTER OF THE CORRECT ANSWER IN THE SPACE AT THE RIGHT.*

1. Subgingival calculus occurs below the gingival margin and can be _____ in color because of subgingival bleeding?
   A. Red   B. Grey   C. Black   D. Yellow

   1.____

2. In which of the following procedures could the patient be placed in an upright position?
   A. Composite procedure
   B. Removal of a posterior tooth
   C. Taking a diagnostic impression
   D. Polishing the teeth after a prophylaxis

   2.____

3. Which of the following would be the MOST common indication for placing pit and fissure sealants?
   A. Posterior teeth with deep pits and fissures
   B. All erupted permanent molars and premolars
   C. Posterior teeth with small areas of early caries
   D. As a preventative measure for partially erupted teeth

   3.____

4. What microorganism must be present for caries formation to begin?
   A. Streptococcus pneumoniae   B. Klebsiella pneumoniae
   C. Candida albicans   D. Streptococcus mutans

   4.____

5. Which of the following is the MOST common form of fluoride used with the rigid tray system?
   A. Sodium fluoride   B. Stannous fluoride paste
   C. Liquid fluoride supplements   D. Acidulated phosphate fluoride gel

   5.____

6. Which of the following statements are TRUE regarding a vulcanite bur?
   A. It smooths roughness in metals.
   B. It grossly reduces an acrylic prosthesis.
   C. It grossly reduces a metal prosthesis.
   D. It polishes acrylic prosthesis with pumice.

   6.____

7. What type of curette has two cutting edges?
   A. Sickle   B. Gracey   C. Kirkland   D. Universal

   7.____

8. What type of file is recommended for canal enlargement?
   A. Pesso   B. Broach   C. Reamer   D. Hedstrom

   8.____

9. The main component in the liquid of zinc phosphate is
   A. zinc oxide
   B. acetic acid
   C. phosphoric acid
   D. hydrogen peroxide

10. Which supplemental material is contraindicated under composite resins and glass ionomer restorations?
    A. Varnish
    B. Etchant
    C. Dentin sealer
    D. Calcium hydroxide

11. Calcium hydroxide is typically placed on what structure of the tooth?
    A. Pulp   B. Dentin   C. Enamel   D. Cementum

12. Which of the following is the technical term for a Class III occlusion?
    A. Distoclusion
    B. Malocclusion
    C. Mesioclusion
    D. Functional occlusion

13. What type of impression material should NOT be mixed while wearing latex gloves?
    A. Polyether
    B. Polysulfide
    C. Hydrocolloid
    D. Condensation silicone

14. Which of the following is the type of fixed prosthesis that only has one abutment?
    A. Partial denture
    B. Maryland bridge
    C. Cantilever bridge
    D. Temporary bridge

15. The rounded raised area on the cervical third of the lingual surface of anterior teeth is referred to as
    A. abrasion   B. mamelon   C. cingulum   D. imbrication

16. Which of the following is an absorbable suture material?
    A. Silk   B. Nylon   C. Plain catgut   D. Polyester fiber

17. Sealant material should NOT be stored in proximity to any products containing which of the following?
    A. Eugenol
    B. Acrylate
    C. BIS-GMA
    D. Sodium bicarbonate

18. Which of the following is a treatment that is used as an attempt to save the pulp and encourage the formation of dentin at the site of an injury?
    A. Pulpotomy
    B. Pulpectomy
    C. Apicoectomy
    D. Pulp capping

19. Which of the following cements has an acidic quality that may be irritating to the pulp?
    A. Glass ionomer
    B. Zinc phosphate
    C. Zinc carboxylate
    D. Zinc oxide eugenol

20. What level of consciousness is a patient at during general anesthesia?
    A. Stage I B. Stage II C. Stage III D. Stage IV

21. When setting up an instrument tray or cassette with instruments, how should the instruments be set up?
    A. From right to left
    B. From left to right
    C. From top to bottom
    D. From bottom to top

22. The assistant's stool should be positioned 4-6 inches
    A. below the dentist
    B. above the dentist
    C. away from the patient
    D. above the patient

23. A base is placed in which location of a cavity preparation?
    A. Cavity wall
    B. Pulpal floor
    C. Proximal wall
    D. Enamel margin

24. Zinc oxide eugenol should be prepared on what type of mixing pad?
    A. Glass
    B. Plastic
    C. Ceramic tile
    D. Treated paper pad

25. Which of the following lines refers to developmental horizontal lines on anterior teeth?
    A. Incisal B. Oblique C. Marginal D. Imbrication

26. Under what condition can a post-extraction dressing be used?
    A. Only after 3rd molar extractions
    B. When there is loss of the blood clot
    C. Any time after a surgical incision
    D. When blood begins to ooze from the alveolus

27. Which medical condition, illustrated in the image at the right, is characterized by the mandible being located ahead of the maxilla?
    A. Retrusion
    B. Prognathism
    C. Micrognathism
    D. Macrognathism

28. Which of the following refers to a living jaw bone naturally growing around an implant?
    A. Osteomalacia
    B. Osteomyelitis
    C. Osseointegration
    D. Osteogenesis

29. Which restorative material releases fluoride?
    A. Glass ionomer   B. Amalgam   C. Ceramic   D. Cast-gold

    29.____

30. What type of dentin forms throughout the life of the tooth, resulting in a narrowing of the pulp chamber?
    A. Primary   B. Secondary   C. Reparative   D. Constrictive

    30.____

KEY (CORRECT ANSWERS)

1.	C	11.	B	21.	B
2.	C	12.	C	22.	B
3.	D	13.	D	23.	B
4.	D	14.	C	24.	A
5.	D	15.	C	25.	D
6.	B	16.	C	26.	B
7.	D	17.	A	27.	B
8.	D	18.	D	28.	C
9.	C	19.	B	29.	A
10.	A	20.	C	30.	B

TEST 4

DIRECTIONS: Each question or incomplete statement is followed by several suggested answers or completions. Select the one that BEST answers the question or completes the statement. *PRINT THE LETTER OF THE CORRECT ANSWER IN THE SPACE AT THE RIGHT.*

1. What feature do newly erupted central and lateral incisors have on the incisal edge? 1.____
   A. Abrasions   B. Mamelons   C. Cingula   D. Imbrications

2. Pain is transmitted through dentin through 2.____
   A. nerves
   B. dentin fibers
   C. dentin tubules
   D. odontoblasts

3. What dental instruments are more commonly referred to by a number rather than a name? 3.____
   A. Pliers
   B. Mirrors
   C. Excavators
   D. Restorative instruments

4. What type of injection technique will a dentist MOST commonly use for maxillary teeth? 4.____
   A. Nerve block
   B. Field block
   C. Infiltration
   D. Subgingival

5. The area or bump found just behind the third molar is referred to as 5.____
   A. tuberosity
   B. alveolar ridge
   C. alveolar socket
   D. retro molar pad

6. The band of connective tissue found next to the bicuspids and lips is referred to as 6.____
   A. labia   B. mucosa   C. frenum   D. alveolar ridge

7. Which tooth has a fifth cusp called the Cusp of Carabelli? 7.____
   A. Maxillary first molar
   B. Maxillary second molar
   C. Mandibular first bicuspid
   D. Mandibular first molar

8. A tofflemire and matrix band is used to form a wall on which cavity classification? 8.____
   A. Class II   B. Class III   C. Class IV   D. Class V

9. When using a rubber dam, which size hole is typically used for a first molar? 9.____
   A. 1   B. 2   C. 3   D. 4

10. If a patient takes a large amount of salicylates, which of the following is MOST likely to be affected?
    A. Sensitivity to antibiotics
    B. Tolerance to pain
    C. Bleeding and clotting time
    D. Tolerance to general anesthesia

11. If an error is made on a clinical record entry, what should be done to correct the error?
    A. Circle the incorrect entry in red
    B. Erase the error and rewrite the entry correctly
    C. Mark through the incorrect entry so that it cannot be read
    D. Draw one line through the incorrect entry and initial and write the correct entry below

12. When assisting during oral surgery, which of the following actions should be avoided?
    A. Flushing the area with water
    B. Wiping oral tissue with gauze
    C. Blowing air to clear the socket
    D. Suctioning the anesthetized area

13. Control of saliva from the parotid duct can be accomplished by placing a cotton roll in what location?
    A. In the vestibule opposite of the maxillary anterior teeth
    B. In the vestibule opposite of the maxillary second molar
    C. In the vestibule opposite of the mandibular second molar
    D. On the lingual side of the mandibular arch under the tongue

14. Which of the following conditions can occur if excess cement remains on the cervical margin after cementation of a crown?
    A. Inflammation of the interdental papillae
    B. Lateral movement of the adjacent tooth
    C. Increase occurrence of subgingival caries
    D. Fracture of the cervical margin of the preparation

15. In selecting an impression tray for a preliminary maxillary impression, the tray should extend posteriorly
    A. behind the tuberosity
    B. beyond the hamular process
    C. to the fauces
    D. to the junction of the hard and soft palates

16. Nitrous oxide analgesia is normally contraindicated for patients with
    A. hypertension
    B. diabetes
    C. nasal congestion
    D. a sensitive gag reflex

17. For what reason would wax be placed along the facial periphery of the maxillary impression tray?
    A. Increased comfort for the patient
    B. To assure registration of the tuberosities
    C. To achieve greater detail of the hard palate
    D. To obtain registration of the mucobuccal attachments

18. In order to achieve maximum effectiveness, when should pit and fissure sealants be placed?
    A. After placement of restorations
    B. After proximal surface becomes carious
    C. Prior to eruption of permanent dentition
    D. After eruption of entire occlusal surface

19. In which area of the dentition is plaque MOST likely to accumulate?
    A. Incisal surfaces
    B. Buccal surfaces
    C. Occlusal surfaces
    D. Proximal spaces

20. To ensure adequate extension of the impression when seating the mandibular impression tray for diagnostic casts, the dental assistant should instruct the patient to
    A. open mouth very wide
    B. raise the mandible
    C. elevate the tongue
    D. drop the chin to the chest

21. Which of the following refers to the grating sound heard in a patient with temporomandibular joint disorder?
    A. Trismus   B. Rales   C. Crepitus   D. Bruits

22. Which of the following bur/handpiece combinations would MOST often be used for removing the carious dentin from the cavity preparation?
    A. #4 bur in a low-speed handpiece
    B. #56 bur in a high-speed handpiece
    C. #330 bur in a high-speed handpiece
    D. #702 bur in a low-speed handpiece

23. When assisting a dentist using a high-speed handpiece during a tooth preparation, what is the PRIMARY purpose for using the air/water syringe?
    A. To keep the mirror clean
    B. To eliminate the need for a cuspidor
    C. To blow debris away from the operating area
    D. To keep the operating area from overheating

24. When a right-handed dentist is preparing the occlusal of tooth #14, the dental assistant is responsible for retracting what area of the patient's face?
    A. Tongue   B. Lower lip   C. Left cheek   D. Right cheek

25. What dental specialty deals with the removal of pulp?
    A. Endodontics
    B. Periodontics
    C. Orthodontics
    D. Prosthodontics

26. Which of the following cements possess anticariogenic properties?
    A. Zinc phosphate
    B. Glass ionomer
    C. Polycarboxylate
    D. Zinc oxide eugenol

27. Which of the following is the activating compound for a visible light curing system? 27.____
    A. Ubiquinone
    B. Camphorquinone
    C. Hydroquinone
    D. Potassium oxide

28. What type of cement is extensively used for attachment of orthodontic brackets to teeth? 28.____
    A. Resin
    B. Silicate
    C. Copper oxide
    D. Glass ionomer

29. What type of cement has antibacterial properties? 29.____
    A. Polycarboxylate
    B. Zinc phosphate
    C. Copper oxide
    D. Zinc oxide eugenol

30. Which part of an amalgam restoration has the HIGHEST mercury concentration? 30.____
    A. Pulpal area
    B. Marginal area
    C. Center of the restoration
    D. Proximal surface of the restoration

KEY (CORRECT ANSWERS)

1. B	11. D	21. C
2. B	12. C	22. A
3. A	13. B	23. A
4. C	14. A	24. C
5. A	15. A	25. A
6. C	16. C	26. B
7. A	17. D	27. B
8. A	18. A	28. A
9. D	19. D	29. C
10. C	20. C	30. B

EXAMINATION SECTION

TEST 1

DIRECTIONS: Each question or incomplete statement is followed by several suggested answers or completions. Select the one that BEST answers the question or completes the statement. *PRINT THE LETTER OF THE CORRECT ANSWER IN THE SPACE AT THE RIGHT.*

1. What type of radiograph is illustrated in the image shown at the right?
    A. Periapical
    B. Bitewing
    C. Pericoronal
    D. Occlusal

    1.____

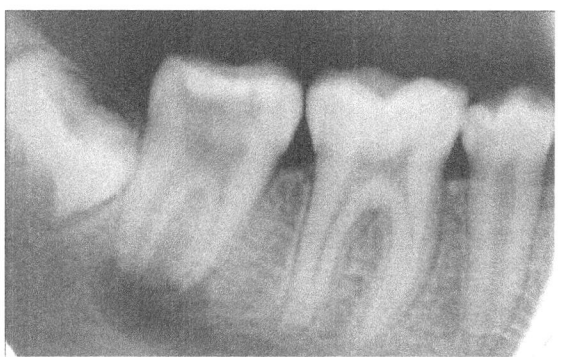

2. Which of the following types of radiation has high linear energy transfer and the potential for causing the greatest amount of radiation related tissue damage?
    A. X-rays
    B. Positrons
    C. Beta radiation
    D. Alpha radiation

    2.____

3. What type of radiograph is illustrated in the image shown at the right?
    A. Periapical
    B. Bitewing
    C. Pericoronal
    D. Occlusal

    3.____

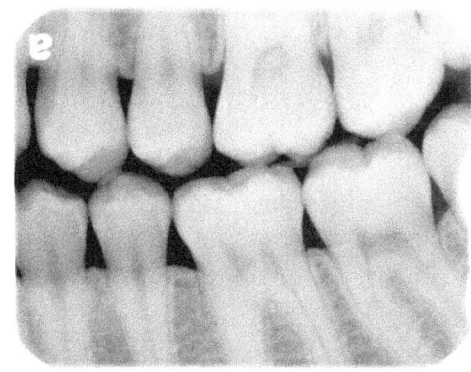

4. What type of radiograph is illustrated in the image shown at the right?
    A. Occlusal
    B. Panoramic
    C. Cephalometric
    D. Periapical

    4.____

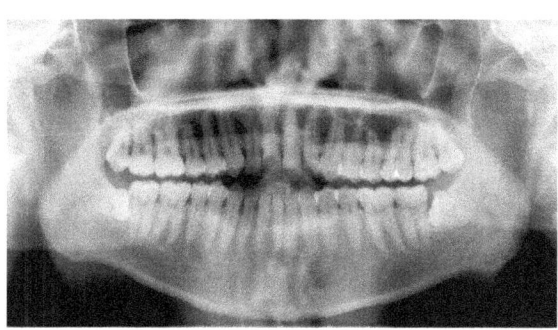

17

5. In the construction of an x-ray tube, what is the function of a step-down transformer?
   Convert the line current of _____ volts to less than _____.
   A. 110; 10 volts
   B. 220; 10 volts
   C. 110; 100 amperes
   D. 110; 10 milli-amperes

   5._____

6. What does the "rotating anode" design in an x-ray tube limit?
   A. Heat production at the anode
   B. X-rays that are produced at the anode
   C. Electrons that are produced at the anode
   D. Speed of electrons from cathode to anode

   6._____

7. To a large extent, what is the sharpness of the image determined by?
   A. Shape of the object
   B. Focal spot size
   C. Manufacturer of the x-ray machine
   D. Distance between the anode and the cathode

   7._____

8. The radiographic view illustrated at right is used frequently in orthodontics for study of the growth and development of the head. What view is illustrated?
   A. Occlusal
   B. Panoramic
   C. Lateral cephalometric
   D. Periapical

   8._____

9. When the target film distance is doubled and the film speed and the machine variables remain constant, the exposure time will be
   A. halved
   B. doubled
   C. four-fold increase
   D. four-fold decrease

   9._____

10. Which of the following determines the total amount of radiation generated during a dental radiographic exposure?
    A. MA
    B. kVp
    C. Exposure time
    D. mAs

    10._____

11. Which of the following is the CORRECT position of the occlusal plane during the bisecting technique?
    A. Parallel to the floor
    B. Perpendicular to the floor
    C. Parallel to the midsagittal plane
    D. Perpendicular to the midsagittal plane

    11._____

12. An insufficient amount of vertical angulation will produce an image that appears
    A. elongated
    B. mottled
    C. foreshortened
    D. overlapped

13. Which of the following would be APPROPRIATE when taking intraoral and panoramic exposures on children?
    A. Decrease exposure time
    B. Increase exposure time
    C. Decrease kVp
    D. Decrease distance from patient to image receptor

14. Which of the following represents the total number of images that would comprises a full mouth series for an adult?
    A. 8-10 images
    B. 10-15 images
    C. 18-20 images
    D. 20-25 images

15. What type of scatter occurs MOST often with dental radiographs?
    A. Compton
    B. Photoelectric
    C. Electromagnetic
    D. Bremsstrahlung

16. The portion of a processed radiograph that appears dark or black is said to be
    A. overexposed
    B. radiolucent
    C. radiopaque
    D. transparent

17. When viewed on a light source, a dental radiography that demonstrates very dark areas and very light areas is said to have
    A. low contrast
    B. high contrast
    C. low resolution
    D. high resolution

18. Which of the following relationships describes the response of tissues to radiation?
    A. Linear, threshold
    B. Linear, non-threshold
    C. Non-linear, threshold
    D. Non-linear, non-threshold

19. Which of the following is the MOST effective method of reducing patient exposure to radiation?
    A. Round PID
    B. Fast films
    C. Lead aprons
    D. Image receptor holding devices

20. Which of the following BEST describes the target-film distance (TFD)?
    A. Distance between tooth and dental x-ray film
    B. Distance from the source of radiation to the film
    C. Distance from the source of radiation to the tooth
    D. Distance from the source of radiation to the patient's skin

21. Which of the following film characteristics is defined as "the amount of radiation needed to produce a radiograph of standard density"?
    A. Size
    B. Speed
    C. Contrast
    D. Image resolution

    21._____

22. When viewed on a light source, a dental radiograph that demonstrates many shades of gray is said to have
    A. low contrast
    B. high contrast
    C. low density
    D. high density

    22._____

23. For what purpose would a dentist order a panoramic image of the mouth?
    A. Diagnosis of caries
    B. Evaluation of periapical disease
    C. Evaluation of impacted molars
    D. Evaluation of periodontal disease

    23._____

24. For what reason should a patient avoid wearing a thyroid collar during a panoramic image?
    A. Thyroid collars cannot be sterilized.
    B. The thyroid receives a generally low dose of radiation.
    C. Thyroid collars block the x-ray beam and obscures information.
    D. The weight of the collar affects the proper positioning of the patient.

    24._____

25. Which of the following refers to the imaginary line that passes from the bottom of the eye socket through the top of the ear canal?
    A. The orbital plane
    B. The vertebral plane
    C. The midsagittal plane
    D. The Frankfort plane

    25._____

KEY (CORRECT ANSWERS)

1. A
2. D
3. B
4. B
5. D

6. A
7. B
8. C
9. C
10. D

11. A
12. A
13. A
14. C
15. A

16. B
17. B
18. B
19. B
20. B

21. B
22. A
23. C
24. C
25. D

TEST 2

DIRECTIONS: Each question or incomplete statement is followed by several suggested answers or completions. Select the one that BEST answers the question or completes the statement. *PRINT THE LETTER OF THE CORRECT ANSWER IN THE SPACE AT THE RIGHT.*

1. Which of the following electrons has the GREATEST binding energy?
   A. K-shell B. L-shell C. M-shell D. N-shell

2. Which of the following refers to the process through which unstable atoms undergo spontaneous disintegration in an effort to attain a more balanced state?
   A. Excitation B. Ionization C. Radioactivity D. Stabilization

3. Which of the following regulates the flow of electrical current to the filament of the x-ray tube?
   A. Low-voltage circuit
   B. High-voltage circuit
   C. Low-voltage transformer
   D. High-voltage transformer

4. The kilovoltage range for the majority of dental x-ray machines is
   A. 50-60 kV
   B. 60-70 kV
   C. 65-100 kV
   D. greater than 100 kV

5. A diagnostic image is produced using 90 kVp and 0.25 seconds. What exposure time is needed to produce the same image at 75 kVp?
   A. 0.50 seconds
   B. 0.75 seconds
   C. 1.00 seconds
   D. 1.25 seconds

6. In which of the following locations does thermionic emission occur?
   A. Positive anode
   B. Positive cathode
   C. Negative anode
   D. Negative cathode

7. Which of the following is the recommended size of the beam at the patient's face?
   A. 2.75 in. B. 3.25 in. C. 3.50 in. D. 4.00 in.

8. Which of the following is defined as variation in the true size and shape of the object being radiographed?
   A. Distortion B. Resolution C. Sharpness D. Magnification

9. _____ mrads is the average dose of background radiation received by an individual in the United States.
   A. 0-100 B. 50-100 C. 150-300 D. 200-500

10. Which of the following refers to unsharpness or blurred lines seen on a radiographic image?
    A. Resolution B. Distortion C. Penumbra D. Interference

11. What is the purpose of a filter in the dental x-ray tubehead?
    A. Remove low-energy x-rays
    B. Decrease the mean energy of the beam
    C. Reduce the size and shape of the beam
    D. Reduce the dose of radiation to the thyroid gland

12. Which of the following refers to the capability of a receptor to reproduce distinct outlines of an object?
    A. Distortion   B. Sharpness   C. Resolution   D. Magnification

13. Dental film that is placed inside the mouth and used to examine the teeth and supporting structures is referred to as _____ film.
    A. perioral   B. interoral   C. extraoral   D. intraoral

14. _____ effects refers to radiation injuries that are not evident in the irradiated person but occur in future generations.
    A. Stochastic   B. Non-stochastic
    C. Somatic   D. Genetic

15. Incorrect horizontal angulation will result in what type of images?
    A. Mottled   B. Overlapped   C. Elongated   D. Foreshortened

16. Which of the following would be an example of a stochastic effect of radiation?
    A. Erythema   B. Cancer
    C. Cataract formation   D. Hair loss

17. Which of the following intensifying screens emits green light and must be used with green-sensitive film?
    A. Phosphor   B. Rare earth
    C. Calcium tungstate   D. Sodium tungstate

18. Which of the following is the milliamperage range used in dental radiography?
    A. 1-5 mA   B. 4-10 mA
    C. 7-15 mA   D. Greater than 15 mA

19. Which of the following plates is used as a collimator in dental radiography?
    A. Lead   B. Aluminum   C. Copper   D. Calcium

20. Which exposure factor has a direct influence on the contrast of a dental radiograph?
    A. mA   B. kVp
    C. Exposure time   D. Subject thickness

21. All of the following would appear radiolucent on a dental radiograph EXCEPT
    A. air   B. bone   C. dental pulp   D. dental caries

22. Which of the following types of cells is radioresistant?
    A. Epithelial
    B. Immature bone
    C. Mature bone
    D. Immature reproductive

23. All of the following would appear radiopaque on a dental radiograph EXCEPT
    A. dentin
    B. enamel
    C. amalgam
    D. periodontal ligament space

24. If the dental radiographic image contained the appropriate density, which of the following would appear gray?
    A. Air
    B. Bone
    C. Dentin
    D. Soft tissue

25. In order to minimize dimensional distortion, the x-ray beam and tooth must be _____ to one another.
    A. parallel
    B. adjacent
    C. perpendicular
    D. at a 45-degree angle

KEY (CORRECT ANSWERS)

1.	A		11.	A
2.	C		12.	B
3.	A		13.	D
4.	C		14.	D
5.	A		15.	B
6.	C		16.	B
7.	A		17.	B
8.	A		18.	C
9.	C		19.	A
10.	C		20.	B

21. B
22. C
23. D
24. D
25. C

TEST 3

DIRECTIONS: Each question or incomplete statement is followed by several suggested answers or completions. Select the one that BEST answers the question or completes the statement. *PRINT THE LETTER OF THE CORRECT ANSWER IN THE SPACE AT THE RIGHT.*

1. To what dental structure is the arrow indicating in the image shown at the right?
   A. Enamel
   B. Dentin
   C. Dentinoenamel junction
   D. Lamina dura

   1.____

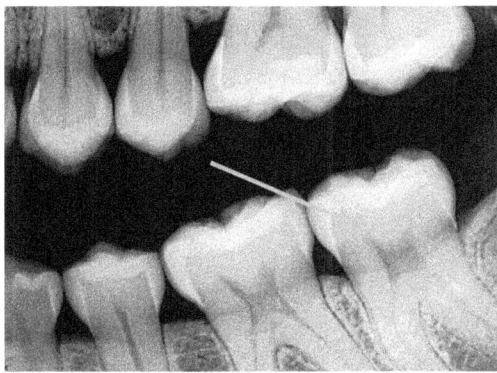

2. To what dental structure is the arrow indicating in the image shown at the right?
   A. Trabeculae
   B. Medullary space
   C. Pulp canal
   D. Pulp chamber

   2.____

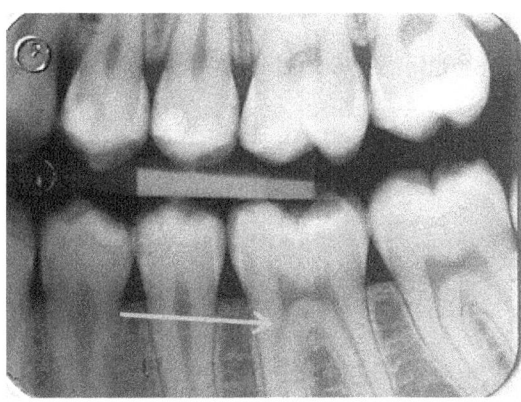

3. Which of the following is an imaginary 3-D horseshoe-shaped zone used to focus panoramic radiographs?
   A. Orbital plane
   B. Vertebral plane
   C. Focal trough
   D. Frankfort plane

   3.____

4. When using the bisecting technique, the imaginary angle that is bisected is formed between the long axis of the tooth and which structure?
   A. Long axis of the PID
   B. Horizontal axis of the film
   C. Long axis of the film
   D. Horizontal axis of the tubehead

   4.____

5. Which type of exposure enables viewing of an area in three planes?
   A. Digital radiography
   B. Computed tomography
   C. Panoramic projection
   D. Cephalometric projection

   5.____

6. When exposing intraoral radiographs, if the patient's right in on your left, where will the identification dot on the film be positioned?
Facing _____ the incisal/occlusal.
   A. out and toward
   B. out and away from
   C. in and toward
   D. in and away from

7. Which regressive alteration of tooth structure appears radiolucent and occurs within the crown or roots of a tooth?
   A. Internal resorption
   B. External resorption
   C. Pathologic resorption
   D. Physiologic resorption

8. Which structure would NOT be seen as a maxillary landmark on a panoramic film?
   A. Incisive canal
   B. Styloid process
   C. Mental foramen
   D. External auditory meatus

9. Using faster F-speed film, a single intraoral film results in a surface skin exposure of _____ milliroentgens.
   A. 1.25
   B. 12.5
   C. 100
   D. 250

10. Which landmark would be found in the mandibular molar exposure?
    A. Inverted Y
    B. Mylohyoid ridge
    C. Mental foramen
    D. External oblique ridge

11. Which of the following body tissues is the MOST sensitive to radiation exposure?
    A. Lymph nodes
    B. Bone marrow
    C. Blood vessels
    D. Thyroid gland

12. What is the MAXIMUM permissible dose of radiation of occupationally exposed workers?
    A. 2 rem/yr
    B. 5 rem/yr
    C. 10 rem/yr
    D. 25 rem/yr

13. Which radiograph shows the bony and soft tissue areas of the facial profile?
    A. Bitewing
    B. Periapical
    C. Panoramic
    D. Cephalometric

14. Which pathologic condition would appear radiopaque on a radiograph?
    A. Infection
    B. Cyst
    C. Tumor
    D. Salivary stone

15. Which radiographic exposure is the view of choice for an intraoral examination of the large areas of the upper and lower jaw?
    A. Occlusal
    B. Bitewing
    C. Periapical
    D. Panoramic

16. Which radiographic exposure is the view of choice for an extraoral examination of the upper and lower jaw?
    A. Occlusal
    B. Bitewing
    C. Periapical
    D. Panoramic

17. What type of radiolucent lesion is characterized by a localized mass of granulation tissue around the apex of a non-vital tooth?
    A. Pulp stone
    B. Odontoma
    C. Amalgam tattoo
    D. Periapical granuloma

17.____

18. How would a completed root canal appear on a processed radiograph?
    A. Elongated
    B. Foreshortened
    C. Radiopaque
    D. Radiolucent

18.____

19. Which of the following statements is FALSE regarding a bitewing radiograph?
    A. The film is placed in the mouth parallel to the crowns of both the upper and lower teeth.
    B. The film is stabilized when the patient bites on the bitewing tab or bitewing film holder.
    C. The central ray of the x-ray beam is directed through the contacts of the teeth using a vertical angulation of +40 degrees.
    D. The bitewing radiograph is a method used to examine the interproximal surfaces of the teeth.

19.____

20. What exposure area will result in the "herringbone effect"?
    A. Film reversal
    B. Collimator cutoff
    C. Overlapped films
    D. Improper film placement

20.____

21. Divergence of the x-ray beam is reduced by using which of the following?
    A. The short cone technique
    B. The paralleling technique
    C. The bisecting technique
    D. An 8-inch PID

21.____

22. What type of image artifact is illustrated by the arrows in the image shown at the right?
    A. Elongation
    B. Ghost image
    C. Foreshortening
    D. Overlapping

22.____

23. Which of the following BEST describes the appearance of bone on a radiograph?
    A. All bones appear radiopaque.
    B. All bones appear radiolucent.
    C. Cortical bone appears radiopaque; cancellous bone appears radiolucent.
    D. Cortical bone appears radiolucent; cancellous bone appears radiopaque.

23.____

24. The inverted Y landmark is composed of which two structures?
    A. Floor of orbit and floor of maxillary sinus
    B. Junction of the right and left nasal cavities
    C. Floor of orbit and anterior border of maxillary sinus
    D. Inferior border of the nasal cavity and anterior border of maxillary sinus

25. What is the PROPER method for mounting radiographs?
    Radiographs should be mounted
    A. as if you were facing the patient
    B. with the dot toward the distal
    C. with the dot toward the mesial
    D. as if you were looking the same way as the patient

KEY (CORRECT ANSWERS)

1.	B	11.	B
2.	C	12.	B
3.	C	13.	D
4.	C	14.	D
5.	B	15.	A
6.	A	16.	D
7.	A	17.	D
8.	C	18.	C
9.	C	19.	C
10.	D	20.	A

21.	B
22.	B
23.	A
24.	D
25.	A

TEST 4

DIRECTIONS: Each question or incomplete statement is followed by several suggested answers or completions. Select the one that BEST answers the question or completes the statement. *PRINT THE LETTER OF THE CORRECT ANSWER IN THE SPACE AT THE RIGHT.*

1. If the patient is properly positioned in the panoramic machine, they should feel
   A. comfortable and relaxed
   B. like they are perfectly upright
   C. like they are leaning forward
   D. like they will fall backwards

   1.____

2. A white, inverted V-shaped radiopacity on the bottom of the film is MOST likely caused by which of the following?
   A. Damaged cassette
   B. Lead apron artifact
   C. Ghost image of hyoid bone
   D. Ghost image of metal jewelry

   2.____

3. Which of the following describes the relationship of the central ray to the film in the paralleling technique?
   A. 75 degrees to film
   B. 65 degrees to film and long axis of tooth
   C. 20 degrees to film long axis of tooth
   D. 90 degrees to film and long axis of tooth

   3.____

4. Which of the following describes the PROPER direction of the central ray in the bisecting technique?
   A. 90 degrees to film
   B. 90 degrees to imaginary bisector
   C. 90 degrees to the film and long axis of tooth
   D. 90 degrees to the long axis of the tooth

   4.____

5. Which of the following is the CORRECT vertical angulation used with a bitewing tab technique?
   A. -10 degrees   B. -20 degrees   C. +10 degrees   D. +15 degrees

   5.____

6. A tungsten target inset into copper is located in what prat of the Coolidge tube?
   A. Filter   B. Anode   C. Cathode   D. Collimator

   6.____

7. What type of radiograph is illustrated in the image shown at the right?
   A. Occlusal
   B. Bitewing
   C. Periapical
   D. Panoramic

   7.____

8. In the radiograph principle, the SLOB rule is defined as "same side movement of the object is lingual and the opposite side movement of the object is _____.
   A. buccal   B. occlusal   C. periapical   D. mesial

9. In children with complete primary dentition and in whom no evidence of disease is found, what type of examination is recommended to assess caries activity?
   A. Occlusal radiograph
   B. Bitewing radiograph
   C. Periapical radiograph
   D. Panoramic radiograph

10. At what age should the FIRST radiographic survey be performed for children?
    A. 3   B. 5   C. 7   D. 9

11. The method of mounting radiographs recommended by the American Dental Association is called the _____ method.
    A. labial   B. mesial   C. periapical   D. occlusal

12. Panoramic units have a tendency to produce images with what type of artifact, particularly in the premolar area?
    A. Mottling
    B. Overlapping
    C. Elongation
    D. Foreshortening

13. Frequently, superimposition of what body part shows up on the anterior position of the panoramic image which is due to the improper positioning of the patient?
    A. Maxillary sinus
    B. Nasal bone
    C. Orbital bone
    D. Spinal column

14. All dental x-ray machines manufactured after what year must meet federal diagnostic equipment performance standards?
    A. 1968   B. 1974   C. 1977   D. 1979

15. The use of lead aprons and thyroid collars can reduce radiation to the thyroid and gonads by what percentage?
    A. 78%   B. 84%   C. 88%   D. 94%

16. Which of the following is one of the major sources of unnecessary exposure to radiation in the dental office?
    A. Old x-ray equipment
    B. Improper shielding
    C. Retaking of x-ray images
    D. Operator too close to x-ray source

17. Ideally, during x-ray exposure, the operator should stand
    A. next to the patient
    B. behind the tube head
    C. at least 6 feet behind the barrier
    D. at least 3 feet from the source of the radiation

18. A film packet placed too far back in the mouth will result in what structures not being imaged?
    A. Anterior   B. Posterior   C. Maxillary   D. Mandibular

19. Which of the following medical conditions is MOST commonly found during a radiographic survey of edentulous ridges?
    A. Cysts
    B. Fractures
    C. Foreign bodies
    D. Retained toots

20. Which of the following digital imaging receptors requires a scanning process to digitize/view the image?
    A. Charge-coupled device
    B. Photostimulable phosphor plate
    C. Fiber optically coupled sensor
    D. Complimentary metal oxide conductor

21. In which area is the film normally positioned vertically?
    A. Mandibular molars
    B. Maxillary canines
    C. Mandibular premolars
    D. Maxillary third molars

22. In digital intraoral radiography, which of the following errors can be corrected without retaking the image?
    A. Cone cuts
    B. Overlapping
    C. Crowns cut off
    D. Film placement

23. When digital receptors are compared to E-speed film, intraoral digital radiography can achieve how much reduction in radiation exposure?
    A. 30-40%   B. 40-50%   C. 50-60%   D. 60-70%

24. In digital radiography, what method can be used to adjust the contrast of an image?
    A. Altering the brightness
    B. Redistributing the gray levels
    C. Reversing the image black to white
    D. Filtering the image to remove noise

25. What method should be used to determine vertical angulation in an edentulous patient?
    A. Estimating the long axis of the ridge
    B. Estimating the sagittal axis of the ridge
    C. Measuring the width of the ridge
    D. Directing the central ray parallel to the ridge

KEY (CORRECT ANSWERS)

1. D
2. B
3. D
4. B
5. C

6. B
7. A
8. A
9. B
10. A

11. A
12. B
13. D
14. B
15. D

16. C
17. C
18. A
19. D
20. B

21. B
22. D
23. C
24. B
25. A

EXAMINATION SECTION
TEST 1

DIRECTIONS: Each question or incomplete statement is followed by several suggested answers or completions. Select the one that BEST answers the question or completes the statement. *PRINT THE LETTER OF THE CORRECT ANSWER IN THE SPACE AT THE RIGHT.*

1. Which of the following is an antimicrobial rinse used to reduce the number of microorganisms before a dental procedure or periodontal treatment?
   A. Monosodium glutamate
   B. Disodium phosphate
   C. Chlorhexidine gluconate
   D. Monohexyl phthalate

   1.____

2. OSHA requires that employers provide employees with what vaccine at no charge?
   A. Influenza
   B. Hepatitis B
   C. Pneumonia
   D. Measles, mumps, and rubella

   2.____

3. In order to be effective, immersion of instruments in glutaraldehyde for high-level sterilization must be maintained for what time period?
   A. 2 hours   B. 6 hours   C. 10 hours   D. 12 hours

   3.____

4. Members of which of the following species of bacteria are the MOST prominent in saliva?
   A. Vaillonella
   B. Actinomyces
   C. Streptococcus
   D. Staphylococcus

   4.____

5. Which of the following is a powerful oxidizing agent that inactivates bacteria and many viruses by oxidizing free sulfhydryl groups?
   A. Phenol   B. Alcohol   C. Chlorine   D. Formaldehyde

   5.____

6. Which of the following is the PROPER time and temperature for autoclaving?
   A. 89°F for 30 minutes
   B. 250°F for 15-20 minutes
   C. 350°F for 1 hour
   D. 450°F for 5 minutes

   6.____

7. What type of pathogens provide the ultimate test for efficacy of sterilization?
   A. Fungi   B. Viruses   C. Bacteria   D. Spore forming

   7.____

8. Which of the following represents the GREATEST risk for blood-borne infection among health care workers?
   A. Tuberculosis
   B. Hepatitis B virus
   C. Hepatitis C virus
   D. Human immunodeficiency virus

   8.____

9. All of the following bacteria may be etiologically related to dental caries EXCEPT
    A. Streptococcus mutans
    B. Lactobacillus casei
    C. Actinomyces israeli
    D. Actinobacillus actionmycetemcomitans

10. Which of the following is the principal oral site for the growth of spirochetes, fusobacteria, and other gram-negative anaerobes?
    A. Saliva
    B. Calculi
    C. The gingival margin
    D. The gingival sulcus

11. A microorganism that settles on the top layer of skin and is removed by handwashing is referred to as
    A. transient flora
    B. transient pathogen
    C. topical flora
    D. topical pathogen

12. What type of gloves should be worn when disposing of a needle?
    A. Sterile   B. Non-sterile   C. Utility   D. Over

13. What type of disinfectant should be used after treating an HIV-positive patient?
    A. Bactericidal   B. Fungicidal   C. Virucidal   D. Bacteriostatic

14. What is the size of a particle that can be inhaled?
    A. Less than 10 microns
    B. 10-15 microns
    C. 15-20 microns
    D. Greater than 20 microns

15. How frequently must sterilization equipment be biologically monitored?
    A. Hourly   B. Daily   C. Weekly   D. Monthly

16. After proper ultrasonic usage, the dental instruments are considered to be
    A. pre-cleaned
    B. decontaminated
    C. disinfected
    D. sterilized

17. Periodontal scalers are examples of what type of instrument?
    A. Super-critical
    B. Critical
    C. Semi-critical
    D. Non-critical

18. For what time period should the air/water syringe be flushed between patients?
    A. 20-30 seconds
    B. 30-60 seconds
    C. 60-90 seconds
    D. 90-120 seconds

19. An inanimate object of substance capable of carrying microbes and transferring them from one individual to another is referred to as
    A. prion   B. fomite   C. pathogen   D. carcinogen

20. According to the Centers for Disease Control and Prevention, effective handwashing should last for approximately what time period? 20.____
    A. 30-60 seconds   B. 1-2 minutes   C. 2-6 minutes   D. 6-8 minutes

21. Which of the following is the PRIMARY active ingredient in the solution used for unsaturated chemical vapor sterilization? 21.____
    A. Water   B. Xylene   C. Alcohol   D. Formaldehyde

22. Biological indicators for monitoring an autoclave or an unsaturated chemical vapor unit contain spores of which of the following? 22.____
    A. Streptococcus mutans
    B. Baccilus atrophaesus
    C. Mycobacterium tuberculosis
    D. Geobacillus stearothermophilus

23. The material in dental waterlines responsible for contaminating the treatment water is commonly referred to as microbial 23.____
    A. biofilm   B. bioburden   C. biowaste   D. biohazard

24. Which organization is responsible for regulating sterilization packaging material in the United States? 24.____
    A. American Dental Association
    B. Environmental Protection Agency
    C. Food and Drug Administration
    D. Occupational Safety and Health Administration

25. What agency regulates the registration of medical/dental disinfectants? 25.____
    A. American Dental Association
    B. Environmental Protection Agency
    C. Food and Drug Administration
    D. Occupational Safety and Health Administration

KEY (CORRECT ANSWERS)

1.	C	11.	A
2.	B	12.	C
3.	C	13.	C
4.	C	14.	A
5.	C	15.	C
6.	B	16.	A
7.	D	17.	B
8.	C	18.	A
9.	D	19.	B
10.	D	20.	C

21. D
22. D
23. A
24. C
25. B

TEST 2

DIRECTIONS: Each question or incomplete statement is followed by several suggested answers or completions. Select the one that BEST answers the question or completes the statement. *PRINT THE LETTER OF THE CORRECT ANSWER IN THE SPACE AT THE RIGHT.*

1. For which of the following is the growth replication determined by environment? 1.____
   A. Bacteria   B. Fungi   C. Viruses   D. Protozoa

2. Which of the following tend to mutate or change during replication making it very difficult for a host to develop adequate immunity? 2.____
   A. Bacteria   B. Fungi   C. Viruses   D. Protozoa

3. Which of the following occurs when respiratory or salivary secretions containing pathogens such as influenza or tuberculosis are expelled from the body? 3.____
   A. Direct transmission
   B. Indirect transmission
   C. Droplet transmission
   D. Vector-borne transmission

4. Which of the following is commonly used to provide a measure of protection against transmission of the human immunodeficiency virus? 4.____
   A. Iodine
   B. Bleach
   C. Formaldehyde
   D. Glutaraldehyde

5. Cocci are bacteria that are _____-shaped. 5.____
   A. rod   B. round   C. spiral   D. flat

6. Bacteria generally consist of an outer wall containing a liquid called 6.____
   A. cytoplasm   B. protoplasm   C. endoplasm   D. exoplasm

7. Which of the following is the process in which bacteria grow, reproduce, and divide into two new cells? 7.____
   A. Mitosis
   B. Meiosis
   C. Binary fission
   D. Binary fusion

8. Which of the following is a method of disease transmission to a susceptible person by handling contaminated instruments or by touching contaminated surfaces? 8.____
   A. Direct transmission
   B. Indirect transmission
   C. Droplet transmission
   D. Vector-borne transmission

9. Which of the following pieces of personal protective equipment should be removed FIRST after the completion of a clinical procedure? 9.____
   A. Mask   B. Gown   C. Gloves   D. Goggles

10. Which of the following is the MOST common route of disease transmission in the dental office?
    A. Direct transmission
    B. Indirect transmission
    C. Droplet transmission
    D. Vector-borne transmission

    10.____

11. The strength of an organism in its ability to produce disease is
    A. purulence
    B. persistence
    C. accordance
    D. virulence

    11.____

12. In what situation would sterile gloves be worn?
    A. Performing a dental examination
    B. Taking a dental radiograph
    C. Performing a dental cleaning
    D. Performing a dental surgical procedure

    12.____

13. When should dental professionals wear masks and protective eyewear to protect the eyes and face?
    A. Anytime there is patient contact
    B. During surgical procedures
    C. While using a high-speed instrument
    D. Anytime blood and saliva spatter can occur

    13.____

14. Training for dental assistants involved in direct patient care must involve which of the following?
    A. Safety, infection control, and hazard communication
    B. Documentation, confidentiality, hand hygiene
    C. Infection control, x-ray techniques, HIPAA
    D. Safety, confidentiality, proper etiquette

    14.____

15. What type of immunity is present at birth?
    A. Active
    B. Passive
    C. Acquired
    D. Inherited

    15.____

16. When a vaccine is administered, the human body forms _____ in response to the vaccine.
    A. antigens
    B. antibodies
    C. pathogens
    D. pyrogens

    16.____

17. What type of immunity is obtained through the administration of a vaccine?
    A. Active natural
    B. Active artificial
    C. Passive natural
    D. Passive artificial

    17.____

18. Which of the following would be an example of a chronic infection?
    A. Influenza
    B. Pneumonia
    C. Common cold
    D. Hepatitis C

    18.____

19. Which of the following would be an example of an acute infection?
    A. Influenza
    B. Tuberculosis
    C. Hepatitis B
    D. Hepatitis C

    19.____

20. Bacteria is commonly identified according to shape; bacilli are bacteria that are _____-shaped.
    A. rod B. round C. spiral D. flat

21. What type of infection results from a defective immune system that cannot defend against pathogens naturally found in the environment?
    A. Latent
    B. Nosocomial
    C. Opportunistic
    D. Pathogenic

22. Which of the following statements is TRUE regarding medical latex or vinyl gloves?
    A. Hands should not be washed prior to gloving.
    B. Hands should not be washed in between patients.
    C. Non-sterile gloves are recommended for surgical procedures.
    D. Non-sterile gloves are recommended for examinations and non-invasive procedures.

23. Which of the following is defined as the absence of pathogens or disease-causing organisms?
    A. Asepti
    B. Antiseptic
    C. Decontaminated
    D. Disinfected

24. Which of the following is defined as a substance that inhibits the growth of bacteria?
    A. Aseptic
    B. Antiseptic
    C. Bacteriostatic
    D. Bacteriocidal

25. At what point can a liquid sterilant or high-level disinfectant achieve complete sterilization?
    A. When the solution is under pressure
    B. When the minimum exposure time is reached
    C. When the solution is heated to 250°F
    D. When used only for longer exposure times

KEY (CORRECT ANSWERS)

1.	A	11.	D
2.	C	12.	D
3.	C	13.	D
4.	B	14.	A
5.	B	15.	D
6.	B	16.	B
7.	C	17.	B
8.	B	18.	D
9.	B	19.	A
10.	A	20.	A

21.	C
22.	D
23.	A
24.	B
25.	D

TEST 3

DIRECTIONS: Each question or incomplete statement is followed by several suggested answers or completions. Select the one that BEST answers the question or completes the statement. *PRINT THE LETTER OF THE CORRECT ANSWER IN THE SPACE AT THE RIGHT.*

1. Which of the following would be acceptable for use as a surface disinfectant in the dental office?
   A. Iodophores B. Ethyl alcohol
   C. Formaldehyde D. Hydrogen peroxide

   1.____

2. Prior to exposing a dental radiograph, in what manner must the treatment area be prepared?
   A. With antiseptic solutions
   B. Using aseptic technique
   C. With low-level disinfectants
   D. By sterilizing the critical instrument

   2.____

3. Manufacturers of autoclaves set them to reach a maximum pressure of 250°F and a pressure of _____ pounds per square inch.
   A. 5-15   B. 15-30   C. 30-45   D. 45-60

   3.____

4. According to guidelines from the Centers for Disease Control and Prevention, which of the following statements is TRUE when transporting a biopsy specimen?
   The specimen should be
   A. placed in a flexible, leak-proof container and marked hazardous
   B. placed in a sturdy, leak-proof container with a biohazard symbol
   C. placed in an OSHA-approved container and handled by a licensed handler
   D. immersed in sterile saline solution, then placed in a sturdy, leak-proof container with a biohazard symbol

   4.____

5. When using which of the following sterilization processes must instruments be absolutely dry or they will rust or develop an ash layer?
   A. Cold sterile B. Chemical vapor
   C. Steam autoclave D. Flash sterilization

   5.____

6. Regarding dental radiography, which of the following would be considered to be a semi-critical instrument?
   A. Thyroid collar B. Exposure button
   C. Control panel D. Film holding device

   6.____

7. Proper ventilation is required for which type of sterilization process?
   A. Chemical vapor B. Immersion disinfection
   C. Steam autoclave D. Flash sterilization

   7.____

8. Which method of sterilization is used to sterilize unwrapped instruments for immediate use?
   A. Chemical vapor
   B. Immersion disinfection
   C. Steam autoclave
   D. Flash sterilization

   8._____

9. Which of the following sterilization processes would be PROPER for sterilizing a mouth mirror?
   A. Chemical immersion
   B. Spray-wipe-spray with surface disinfectant
   C. Autoclave with emulsion
   D. Autoclave without emulsion

   9._____

10. Which of the following sterilization processes would be PROPER for sterilizing an explorer?
    A. Chemical immersion
    B. Spray-wipe-spray with surface disinfectant
    C. Autoclave with emulsion
    C. Autoclave without emulsion

    10._____

11. Which of the following sterilization processes would be PROPER for a saliva ejector?
    A. Chemical immersion
    B. Spray-wipe-spray with surface disinfectant
    C. Autoclave with emulsion
    D. Manufactured for one-time use and should be discarded

    11._____

12. In the dental office, what type of sterilization requires the HIGHEST temperature?
    A. Autoclaving
    B. Chemical vapor
    C. Dry heat sterilization
    D. Ethylene oxide sterilization

    12._____

13. What type of sterilization should be avoided for sterilizing dental burs?
    A. Autoclaving
    B. Chemical vapor sterilization
    C. Chemical liquid sterilization
    D. Flash sterilization

    13._____

14. In the dental office, it is desirable for the instrument processing area to be
    A. outside of the treatment room
    B. dedicated solely to instrument processing
    C. part of the treatment room and dental laboratory
    D. large enough to accommodate several staff members

    14._____

15. Holding solutions are used for which of the following purposes?
    A. Clean instruments
    B. Disinfect instruments
    C. Decontaminate instruments
    D. Prevent debris from drying on instruments

    15._____

16. Which of the following methods of pre-cleaning dental instruments should be avoided?
    A. Hand scrubbing
    B. Automated washer
    C. Ultrasonic cleaning
    D. Placing in holding solution

16._____

17. How often should the ultrasonic cleaner be cleaned and disinfected?
    A. After every load   B. Daily   C. Weekly   D. Monthly

17._____

18. How should instruments be treated after completing a cleaning cycle in the ultrasonic cleaner?
    They should be
    A. deemed fit for use
    B. rinsed with water
    C. placed in the sterilizer
    D. wiped with disinfectant

18._____

19. Which of the following statements is TRUE regarding ultrasonic cleaners?
    A. They clean and sterilize.
    B. They clean and disinfect.
    C. They clean and decontaminate.
    D. They clean and remove debris.

19._____

20. Which of the following is defined as the process that kills disease-causing organisms but not necessarily all microbial life?
    A. Cleaning
    B. Disinfection
    C. Decontamination
    D. Sterilization

20._____

21. Spores of which of the following types of bacteria are used to monitor dry heat sterilizers?
    A. Streptococcus mutans
    B. Baccilus atrophaesus
    C. Mycobacterium tuberculosis
    D. Geobacillus stearothermophilus

21._____

22. There is a vaccine for all of the following medical conditions that may be encountered in dental patients EXCEPT
    A. influenza   B. pneumonia   C. hepatitis B   D. strep throat

22._____

23. In a susceptible person, infection with the Legionella bacteria can lead to which medical condition?
    A. Influenza   B. Pneumonia   C. Hepatitis B   D. Strep throat

23._____

24. According to OSHA guidelines, which of the following actions is ACCEPTABLE prior to placing a contaminated needle into a sharps container?
    A. Cutting the needle
    B. Breaking the needle
    C. Bending the needle
    D. Recapping the needle

24._____

25. Which of the following statements is TRUE regarding infection control in the clinical care environment?
    A. All barriers should be changed on a daily basis.
    B. Isopropyl alcohol should be used to disinfect fixed surfaces.
    C. Fixed surfaces should be made of porous materials.
    D. Carpet and cloth-upholstered furnishings should be avoided.

25._____

KEY (CORRECT ANSWERS)

1.	A	11.	D
2.	B	12.	C
3.	B	13.	D
4.	B	14.	B
5.	B	15.	D
6.	D	16.	A
7.	A	17.	B
8.	D	18.	B
9.	D	19.	D
10.	C	20.	B

21.	B
22.	D
23.	B
24.	D
25.	D

TEST 4

DIRECTIONS: Each question or incomplete statement is followed by several suggested answers or completions. Select the one that BEST answers the question or completes the statement. *PRINT THE LETTER OF THE CORRECT ANSWER IN THE SPACE AT THE RIGHT.*

1. The Organization for Safety Asepsis and Prevention identifies the classification of clinical touch surfaces to include
   A. telephones, stools, and permanent cabinetry
   B. light handles, dental unit controls, and chair switches
   C. unit master switches, permanent cabinetry, and patient charts
   D. instrument trays, handpiece holders, and countertops

   1.____

2. Which of the following is the APPROPRIATE definition for standard precautions?
   A. The use of the same infection control procedures for all types of health care facilities
   B. The concept that considers all patients to have infections caused by a blood-borne pathogen
   C. The use of only infection control procedures formally approved by a government agency
   D. The concept that considers that blood and all patient bodily fluids are infectious

   2.____

3. Which of the following is the BEST time to clean and disinfect a dental prosthesis or impression that will be processed in a dental laboratory?
   A. After it has had time to dry
   B. As soon as it arrives at the dental facility
   C. Prior to inserting into the patient's mouth
   D. As soon as possible after removal from the patient's mouth

   3.____

4. Which of the following is considered to be regulated waste and requires special disposal?
   A. Food
   B. Human tissue
   C. Saliva-soaked gauze
   D. Used anesthetic cartridge

   4.____

5. How often should a member of the dental office team check the contents of the emergency kit to determine that the contents are in place and within the expiration date?
   A. Weekly   B. Monthly   C. Quarterly   D. Bi-annually

   5.____

6. According to the Environmental Protection Agency, wastes are classified as hazardous if they are
   A. ingestible
   B. ignitable
   C. biodegradable
   D. compostable

   6.____

7. Which of the following statements are TRUE regarding waste containers that house potentially infectious materials?
   A. They require special disposal.
   B. They should be in a yellow bag.
   C. They should be labeled as infectious waste.
   D. They should be labeled with a biohazard symbol.

8. Through what method should scrap dental amalgam be collected and stored?
   A. In a clear glass jar
   B. In a designated dry airtight container
   C. In an airtight container containing a disinfectant
   D. In an airtight container with glutaraldehyde

9. Which government agency oversees, regulates, and enforces the disposal of regulated wastes?
   A. Environmental Protection Agency
   B. Centers for Disease Control and Prevention
   C. Food and Drug Administration
   D. Department of Health and Human Services

10. If a dental health worker transfers a small amount of glass ionomer cement for use at the chairside of a patient, under what circumstance would a new label have to be placed on that container?
    A. If the patient was positive for tuberculosis, hepatitis C, or HIV
    B. If there is no MSDS sheet on file for the material
    C. If additional material is required to treat the patient
    D. If the material is not used in its entirety by the end of the shift

11. Which of the following needle recapping methods should be avoided?
    A. One-handed scoop technique
    B. Two-handed scoop technique
    C. Mechanical recapping device
    D. Using any fixed device that allows the operator's hand to remain behind the needle

12. All of the following would be considered a "sharp" EXCEPT
    A. needle
    B. orthodontic wire
    C. metal matrix band
    D. metal matrix retainer

13. Which of the following should be avoided during the use of nitrous oxide during conscious sedation?
    A. Using a scavenger system
    B. Securing the patient's mask
    C. Using a dental dam when applicable
    D. Maintaining a conversation with the patient

14. Distillation of water is a(n) _____ process that may remove volatile chemicals, endotoxins, and some microorganisms.
    A. ionization
    B. purification
    C. sterilization
    D. annihilation

    14.____

15. The transmission of disease through the skin, as with cuts or punctures, is referred to as what type of transmission?
    A. Indirect
    B. Parenteral
    C. Percutaneous
    D. Topical

    15.____

16. Which of the following would be a cause for the sterilization process to fail?
    A. Using paper bags in the steam sterilizer
    B. Using distilled water in the steam sterilizer
    C. Leaving excessive space between packages
    D. Using closed containers in the steam or chemical vapor sterilizer

    16.____

17. An emergency action plan can be communicated to employees orally if the place of business has fewer than how many employees?
    A. 10
    B. 25
    C. 40
    D. 50

    17.____

18. An area in which a pathogen can grow, such as soiled dressings and medical equipment, is referred to as which of the following?
    A. Vector
    B. Vehicle
    C. Fomite
    D. Reservoir

    18.____

19. The interval between the entrance of the pathogen into the body and the appearance of symptoms is known as the
    A. incubation period
    B. prodromal stage
    C. acute stage
    D. inoculation period

    19.____

20. Which of the following refers to microorganisms that are always present but usually do not alter the health of humans?
    A. Transient flora
    B. Resident flora
    C. Topical flora
    D. Persistent flora

    20.____

21. Which of the following are single-celled microscopic animals without a rigid cell wall?
    A. Prions
    B. Protozoa
    C. Fungi
    D. Viruses

    21.____

22. According to the Centers for Disease Control and Prevention, what type of water should be used for surgical procedures?
    A. Bottled
    B. Purified
    C. Distilled
    D. Sterile

    22.____

23. Approximately what percentage of patients with HIV or Hepatitis B show no symptoms and are unaware they are infectious?
    A. 50%
    B. 60%
    C. 70%
    D. 80%

    23.____

24. Dental procedures usually generate particles that average how many microns in diameter?
    A. 1.3
    B. 5.7
    C. 9.6
    D. 12.5

    24.____

25. How often must Bowie-Dick tests be performed when using pre-vacuum sterilizers? 25._____
    A. After each sterilization
    B. Daily
    C. Weekly
    D. Monthly

KEY (CORRECT ANSWERS)

1.	B		11.	B
2.	D		12.	D
3.	D		13.	D
4.	B		14.	B
5.	B		15.	B
6.	B		16.	D
7.	D		17.	A
8.	B		18.	D
9.	A		19.	A
10.	D		20.	B

21. B
22. D
23. D
24. A
25. C

FUNDAMENTALS OF DENTAL ASSISTING

SECTION 1: DIDACTIC EDUCATION: FUNDAMENTALS OF DENTAL ASSISTING

Table 1. Educational Parameters of the Didactic Component of the Fundamentals of Dental Assisting Curriculum		
Unit	Title	Number of Tasks
1	Introduction to the Dental Profession	33
2	Dentistry and the Law	56
3	Dental Terminology	191
4	Preventative Oral Health	53
5	Infection Control	200
6	Patient Management	66
7	Anatomy	80
8	Dental Equipment	50
9	Dental Instruments and Procedures	121
10	Clinical Records	84
11	Oral Pathology	68
12	Emergency Care	60
13	Dental Anesthesia	75
14	Chair-Side Assisting	66
15	Dental Materials	82
16	Introduction to Dental Radiography	190
	Total	1,475

FUNDAMENTALS OF DENTAL ASSISTING

1.0 INTRODUCTION TO THE DENTAL PROFESSION
(I) Number of Tasks to Master = 33
(II) Intended Outcome: Given information about the dental team, specialties, and dental assisting credentials, the student will perform 85% of the following tasks with accuracy on the didactic exam.
(III) Tasks:

1.01 The Dental Team

A. Identify five members of the dental profession:
1. Dentist
2. Dental Assistant
3. Dental Hygienist
4. Business Assistant
5. Dental Laboratory Technician

B. Define the five members of the dental team:
1. Dentist: Leader of the dental team, responsible for all of the treatment and care of the patient.
2. Dental Assistant: Aids the dentist in diagnosis, treatment and dental care.
3. Dental Hygienist: Concerned with the prevention of dental disease, specializing in the cleaning, polishing, and radiographing teeth, periodontal treatment, and patient education.
4. Business Assistant: Responsible for the smooth and efficient operation of the business office.
5. Dental Laboratory Technician: Performs dental lab procedures according to a written prescription of a licensed dentist.

1.02 The Dental Specialties

A. Describe the nine specialty fields of dentistry:
1. Dental Public Health: Involves public/community education to control and prevent disease.
2. Endodontics: Concerned with the cause, diagnosis, prevention, and treatment of diseases and injuries to the pulp and associated structures.
3. Oral and Maxillofacial Radiology: Enhance imaging techniques to locate tumors and infectious diseases of the jaw, assist in trauma cases, and help pinpoint temporomandibular disorders, newest of the specialties.
4. Oral and Maxillofacial Surgery: Involves the diagnosis and surgical treatment of diseases, injuries, and defects of the oral and maxillofacial regions.
5. Oral Pathology: Concerned with the nature of the diseases affecting the oral cavity and adjacent structures. Perform biopsies and work closely with oral surgeons to provide a diagnosis.
6. Orthodontics: Involves the diagnosis, prevention, interception, and treatment of all forms of malocclusion of the teeth and associated structures.

7. Pediatric Dentistry: Concerned with the oral health care of children from birth to adolescence, often dealing with emotional or behavioral problems.
8. Periodontics: Concerned with the diagnosis and treatment of the oral tissues supporting and surrounding the teeth.
9. Prosthodontics: Concerned with the restoration and replacement of natural teeth with artificial replacements.

1.03 Dental Assisting Credentials

A. Define seven acronyms for identification of dental assistants:
1. CDA: Certified Dental Assistant
2. CDPMA: Certified Dental Practice Management Administrator
3. COA: Certified Orthodontic Assistant
4. COSMA: Certified Oral and Maxillofacial Surgery Assistant
5. RDA: Registered Dental Assistant
6. RDAEF: Registered Dental Assistant in Expanded Functions
7. EFDA: Expanded Function Dental Assistant

B. Explain how each of the seven dental assisting credentials may be obtained:
1. CDA: Granted by the Dental Assisting National Board after successful completion of the national certification examination.
2. CDPMA: Granted by the Dental Assisting National Board to recognize successful completion of the specialty examination in dental practice management.
3. COA: Granted by the Dental Assisting National Board to recognize successful completion of the specialty examination on Orthodontics.
4. COMSA: This credential is no longer granted but is still recognized. Granted by the Dental Assisting National Board to recognize successful completion of a specialty examination in oral and maxillofacial surgery.
5. RDA: Given by some states to indicate that specific requirements have been met to practice expanded and advanced functions for that state.
6. RDAEF: Given by some states to indicate that specific requirements have been met to practice expanded and advanced functions in that state.
7. EFDA: Given by some states to indicate specific requirements have been met to practice expanded and advanced functions of that state.

2.0 DENTAL ETHICS AND THE LAW
(I) Number of Tasks to Master = 56
(II) Intended Outcome: Given information about legal, ethical, and risk management considerations, the student will be able to perform 85% of the following tasks on the didactic examination.
(III) Tasks:

2.01 Legal Considerations

A. Identify and give the function of five agencies that regulate dentistry:
   1. State Board of Dentistry
   2. Drug Enforcement Agency
   3. State Board of Pharmacy
   4. Occupational Safety and Health Administration
   5. Environmental Protection Agency

B. Identify current prohibitions specified by Rule 35 of the Idaho Dental Practice Act.

C. Define two types of law that affect dentistry:
   1. Civil Law (i.e., malpractice suit)
      a. Contract Law
      b. Tort Law
   2. Criminal Law (i.e., unlicensed dentistry, fraud)

D. List who may be the subject of a lawsuit:
   1. Initiating Dentist
   2. Dental Assistant
   3. Hygienist

E. State the purpose of professional liability insurance.

F. Explain who owns the dental record.

2.02 Ethical Considerations

A. Define ethical behavior.

B. Define five ethical concepts that are important to a dental assistant:
   1. Confidentiality
   2. Respect for the profession
   3. Respect for fellow staff and dentist
   4. Maintain skills and knowledge
   5. Refrain from services prohibited by state law

2.03 Risk Management Considerations

A. Define risk management.

B. List seven elements of an informed consent:
   1. Description of treatment
   2. Alternatives of treatment
   3. Risk of complications
   4. Prognosis
   5. Cost
   6. Time needed to complete
   7. Age and mental capacity of patient

C. Explain three ways to obtain informed consent:
   1. Implied consent
   2. Verbal consent
   3. Written consent

D. Describe thirteen ways to manage risk:
   1. Informed consent
   2. Review medical history
   3. Emergency preparedness
   4. Clear/Realistic patient expectations
   5. Maintain high level of skill
   6. Adequate patient safety equipment
   7. Disclosure of unexpected events
   8. Comprehensive/accurate treatment record
   9. Never criticize previous treatment
   10. Protect privacy of patient (HIPPA)
   11. Document privacy of patient (HIPPA)
   12. Identify responsibility/obligations in the dentist/patient relationship
   13. How to respond to a threat of malpractice suit

E. List six guidelines for managing chart entries as a legal record:
   1. Keep a separate chart for each patient
   2. Correct errors properly
   3. Make chart entry during patient visit, do not rely on memory
   4. Write legibly, in ink, date and initial each entry
   5. The entry should be complete
   6. Never change or alter the chart after a problem arises

3.0 DENTAL TERMINOLOGY
(I) Number of Tasks to Master = 191
(II) Intended Outcome: Given information about the value of dental terminology, prefixes, word roots, and suffixes, the student will perform the following tasks with 85% accuracy on the didactic examination.
(III) Tasks:

3.01 Dental Prefixes

A. List and define the following 83 dental prefixes:

1.	a-; an-	without, away from, not
2.	ab-	from, away negative, absent
3.	ad-	increase, toward
4.	an-	without, not
5.	ana-	up, throughout
6.	ano-	up
7.	anti-	opposed to, against, counteracting
8.	auto-	self
9.	bi-	two, twice, double
10.	bio-	life
11.	brady-	slow
12.	canth-	corner of the eye

13.	circum-	around
14.	contra-	against, opposed
15.	de-	from, lack of
16.	demi-	half
17.	dens-	tooth
18.	dent-	tooth, teeth
19.	derma-	skin
20.	di-	twice, double
21.	dia-	complete, through
22.	dors-	back
23.	dys-	bad, difficult, painful
24.	e-/ec-	out of, from
25.	ecto-	external, outside
26.	edem/a-	swelling
27.	endo-	within
28.	epi-	over, upper, upon
29.	erythr/o	red
30.	eth/m-	sieve
31.	eti/o	cause
32.	ex-; ex/o	out away from, completely
33.	extra-	beyond, outside
34.	faci/a	face, appearance
35.	fore-	in front of
36.	gene-	origin, beget
37.	hem/a/i	blood
38.	hepa-	liver
39.	homo-	same
40.	hydra-	water
41.	hyo-	U-shaped, horshoe-shaped
42.	hyper-	above, excessive, beyond
43.	hypo-	less than, below, under
44.	idio-	peculiar, one's own
45.	inter-	in the midst, between
46.	intra-	within
47.	infra-	beneath, under, inferior
48.	leuk/o	white
49.	macro-	large
50.	mal-	evil, sickness, disorder, bad, poor
51.	mesi/o	middle
52.	mucos/a	mucus membrane
53.	myel/o	spinal cord, bone marrow
54.	myo-	muscle
55.	neo-	new
56.	necr/a	death, dead
57.	nephr/o	kidney
58.	neuro-	nerve
59.	nutri-	feed, nourish
60.	pan-	all
61.	para-	besides, beyond
62.	peri-	around, about

	63.	poly-	many, much
	64.	post-	behind, after
	65.	pre-	before, in front of
	66.	pseudo-	false
	67.	ptery-	a wing
	68.	ptya/l	spit, saliva
	69.	pyo-	pus
	70.	re-	back, again
	71.	retro-	backwards
	72.	sub-	under, beneath, less normal
	73.	super-	above, superior, beyond
	74.	supra-	above, excessive
	75.	syn-	together, union
	76.	tachy-	fast
	77.	tic-	relation, belonging to
	78.	trans-	across, over, beyond, through
	79.	tri-	three, trice, third
	80.	ventro	body front
	81.	ultra-	beyond, excess
	82.	un-	not
	83.	uni-	one

3.02   Dental Root Words

A. List and define the following 55 dental root words:

1.	alve/o	alveolus (tooth socket bone)
2.	amalg	soft mass
3.	amel/o	tooth, enamel tissue
4.	angio	vessel
5.	ankyl	anchored, crooked
6.	anter/o	before, in front of
7.	apic/o	apex of the root, tip
8.	brux/i/o	chew, grind
9.	bucc	cheek
10.	calcul	small stone, limestone
11.	cardi/o	heart
12.	carcin/o	cancer
13.	cari/es/o	rottenness, decay
14.	cephal/o	head
15.	cheil/o	lip
16.	clavi/o	a club
17.	cocci	round, spherical bacteria
18.	colli	neck
19.	coron/a	crown
20.	cyan/o	blue
21.	cyst	fluid filled sac
22.	cyt	cell
23.	decidu	shedding
24.	dens/t	tooth
25.	di	across, separate apart

26.	diastema/a	space, interval
27.	dist/o	farthest from center
28.	edem/a	swelling
29.	edentul/o	without teeth
30.	erythr/o	red
31.	fluor/o	fluoride
32.	foss/o	shallow depression
33.	frene	frenum, connecting tissue
34.	gingiv	gingival, gum tissue
35.	gloss/o	tongue
36.	halit/o	breath
37.	hem/a/o	blood
38.	incis/o	incisor tooth
39.	infer/o	under, below
40.	labi/o	lip area
41.	lacrim/o	tears
42.	lingu/o	tongue
43.	lip/i/o	fat
44.	lith/o	stone
45.	mandibul/a	lower jaw
46.	mastic/o	chew
47.	maxilla/a/o	upperjaw
48.	melan/o	black
49.	mesi/o	middle, mid-line
50.	muc/o	tissue lining an orifice
51.	my/o	muscle
52.	occlus/o	occlusion, jaw closing
53.	orth/o	straight, proper order
54.	stoma	mouth
55.	tempor/o	temporal bone/joint

3.03 Dental Suffixes

A. List and define the following 52 dental suffixes:

1.	-ac, -ic, -ar	describes or shows relation to
2.	-al	used to indicate connection with
3.	-algia/-esia	pain, suffering
4.	-ia	state of being
5.	-ase	enzyme
6.	-cife	kill
7.	-cise	cut into
8.	-cyte	cell
9.	-dema	swelling
10.	-ectomy	surgical removal
11.	--emia	blood
12.	-eme/-tic/-sis	producing vomiting
13.	-esthesia	sensation
14.	-eum	a place where
15.	-graph/y	picture, recording of a picture
16.	-gram	graph, picture (used in radiology)

17.	-iama	medicine, remedy
18.	-iasis	abnormal condition
19.	-im	not, in, into
20.	-ism	state of, condition
21.	-ist	specialist in, superlative
22.	-it is	inflammation of
23.	-ium	small
24.	-ize	take away, remove
25.	-lar	describing, about
26.	-lith	stone
27.	-logist	specialist
28.	-logy	study of
29.	-lysis	destruction
30.	-nomy	science of
31.	-oid	like, resembling
32.	-ology	study of
33.	-oma	tumor, swelling
34.	-orrhea	flow, excessive flow
35.	-otomy	cutting into, incision into
36.	-osis	abnormal, condition of
37.	-ous	pertaining to, full of
38.	-path/o/y	disease
39.	-phob	fear, dread
40.	-plasty	surgical correction
41.	-pnea	breathing
42.	-rrhage	excessive flow
43.	-rrhea	excessive
44.	-scoli/o	twisted
45.	-scopy	scan, visual exam
46.	-sis	the act of
47.	-stalsis	constriction, contraction
48.	-tic	pertaining to
49.	-tome	cutting instrument
50.	-trophy	development, growth, nourishment
51.	-um	pertaining to
52.	-y	act, result of an act

4.0 PREVENTIVE ORAL HEALTH

(I) Number of Tasks to Master = 53

(II) Intended Outcome: Given information about preventive dentistry, plaque removal, fluoride, and nutrition, the student will be able to perform the following tasks with 85% accuracy on the didactic examination.

(III) Tasks:

4.01 Comprehensive Preventive Dentistry

A. Explain the goal of preventive dentistry.

B. Describe the five parts of a comprehensive preventive dentistry program:
   1. Nutrition
   2. Patient education
   3. Plaque control
   4. Fluoride therapy
   5. Sealants

4.02 Bacterial Plaque

A. Explain the composition of plaque.

B. Explain the three steps of plaque formation:
   1. Pellicle formation nutrition
   2. Bacteria attach to the pellicle
   3. Bacteria multiply and mature

4.03 Dental Calculus

A. Define dental calculus:
   1. Dental calculus is mineralized bacterial plaque. It is a tenacious deposit that forms on the clinical crowns and roots of teeth.

B. List the two types of dental calculus:
   1. Supragingival calculus
   2. Subgingival calculus

4.04 Dental Caries

A. Explain the five stages that must be present for the development of caries:
   1. Cariogenic food, in the form of carbohydrates, are mixed in with the plaque.
   2. Plaque and bacteria mix together and the pH of the plaque becomes more acidic.
   3. Acid formation begins.
   4. Frequent exposure of tooth to acid begins demineralization of the tooth structure.
   5. Caries formation.

B. Define cariogenic:
   1. Producing or promoting tooth decay.

C. List two factors that contribute to dental caries:
   1. A diet high in cariogenic foods
   2. Frequent exposure to sucrose

4.05 Periodontal Disease

A. List the main contributing factor in periodontal disease:
   1. Bacterial plaque

B. List four contributing factors in periodontal disease:
   1. Inadequate plaque control
   2. Lack of patient compliance
   3. Tobacco use
   4. Systemic diseases

4.06 Patient Education

A. Evaluation of patient:
   1. Oral health status and habits
   2. Use appropriate disclosing aids
   3. Provide individualized education plan
   4. Evaluate patients' progress

B. List four factors in toothbrush selection:
   1. Soft bristles
   2. Easily cleaned
   3. Replaceable every 3-4-months
   4. Adapted to individual patient

C. Describe two toothbrushing techniques:
   1. Bass or sulcular brushing technique
   2. Rolling or circular brushing technique

D. List three flossing considerations:
   1. Floss every 24 hours
   2. Most effectively removes plaque between teeth
   3. Choice of type depends on individual patient needs

E. Describe five special interdental aids:
   1. Floss holder
   2. Floss threader
   3. Stimulators
   4. Interproximal brush
   5. Oral irrigation device

4.07 Fluoride

A. Describe two methods of fluoride delivery, advantages, and disadvantages:
   1. Types of systemic
   2. Types of topical

B. Explain the possible dangers of fluoride:
   1. Define dental fluorosis
   2. Overdose

4.08 Nutrition

A. Define cariogenic foods.

B. Describe three effects cariogenic foods have on dental health:
   1. Promotes plaque formation
   2. Promotes tooth decay
   3. Promotes periodontal disease

C. Provide dietary assessment related to dental health.

5.0 INFECTION CONTROL
(I) Number of Tasks to Master = 200
(II) Intended Outcome: Given information about disease transmission, infectious diseases, universal precautions, the treatment room, cleaning, sterilization, disinfecting, disinfectants, hazards, and instrument sterilization, the student will be able to perform the following tasks with 85% accuracy on the didactic examination.
(III) Tasks:

5.01 Disease Transmission

A. Define pathogenic:
   1. Disease causing microorganisms

B. Define spore:
   1. Highly resistant form of bacteria that are able to remain inactive under unfavorable conditions and can become active when conditions are favorable.

C. Define five modes of disease transmission in a dental office:
   1. Direct transmission
   2. Indirect transmission
   3. Splatter or splash
   4. Airborne transmission
   5. Dental water lines

D. List and explain three methods for airborne transmission:
   1. Splatter: Large particles, such as tooth fragments and debris are released into the air during cavity preparations.
   2. Mists: Droplets transported via coughing causing respiratory infections.
   3. Aerosols: Microorganisms are found in the aerosols created by ultrasonic scalers, high-speed handpieces, and the use of air-water syringes.

E. Define cross-examination:
   1. Cross-contamination refers to the spread of microorganisms from one source to another source.

F. List two methods in which cross-contamination can occur:
   1. Person-to-person contact
   2. Person to an inanimate object, and then to another person

G. List three ways to prevent cross-contamination:
   1. Reduction of pathogenic microorganisms
   2. Breaking the chain of disease transmission
   3. Application of universal precautions

5.02 Infectious Diseases

A. List and explain the five types of hepatitis and the route of transmission for each type:
   1. Hepatitis 1: Fecal and oral
   2. Hepatitis B (HBV): Blood, saliva, and body fluids
   3. Hepatitis C: Percutaneous, blood, and contaminated needles
   4. Hepatitis D (Delta): Co-infection with hepatitis B, blood, sexual contact, and perinatal
   5. Hepatitis E: Fecal and oral, contaminated water

B. Explain five types of individuals at risk for contracting hepatitis B:
   1. Patients with active or chronic liver disease
   2. Military populations stationed in countries with a high incidence of hepatitis B
   3. Infants born to HIV-infected mothers
   4. IV drug users
   5. Heterosexually active persons with multiple sexual partners

C. Explain the time interval for administering the hepatitis B vaccine:
   1. Administered in three doses: initial dose and then at one and six months

D. List two types of herpes viruses:
   1. Herpes simplex virus-1
   2. Herpes simplex virus-2

E. List three reasons to postpone treatment for a patient with an active herpetic lesion:
   1. Contiguousness of the lesion
   2. Transfer of the virus to other areas of the face
   3. Irritation to the lesion from dental procedures can prolong healing

F. Define the term HIV
   1. Human immunodeficiency virus

G. List and explain three modes of transmission for HIV:
   1. Perinatal: Transmission across the placenta, during delivery, or breast-feeding
   2. Sexual Contact: Heterosexual or homosexual relations
   3. IV Drug Users: Shared or contaminated needles

H. List four other diseases of concern to dental health workers:
   1. Tuberculosis
   2. Tetanus
   3. Legionnaires'
   4. Measles

5.03 Prevention of Disease Transmission

A. Define the four factors of disease transmission
   1. Virulence
   2. Pathogenic organisms must be present in quantities and concentration sufficient to overtake the body defenses
   3. A susceptible host must be present, one who cannot resist infection
   4. Pathogens must have means of entering the body (portal of entry)

B. Explain eight methods used to prevent disease transmission:
   1. Eliminating or controlling the organisms found in the oral cavity by brushing teeth or rinsing with an antiseptic mouthwash
   2. Interruption of transmission of organisms by the use of rubber dam and high-speed evacuation system
   3. Wearing protective eyewear, gloves and mask (universal precautions)
   4. Sterilization of dental instruments by autoclaving
   5. Use of disposables when possible
   6. Immunization of dental personnel
   7. Avoid procedures on patients with lesions of communicable diseases
   8. Properly store all instruments and materials

5.04 OSHA Bloodborne Pathogens Standard

A. List the components required by the OSHA Bloodborne Pathogen Standards:
   1. Exposure control plan
   2. Standard and Universal Precaution
   3. Categorization of employees
   4. Post exposure management
   5. Employee training
   6. Hepatitis B immunization

B. List OSHA Bloodborne Pathogens Standard Training Requirements:
   1. Epidemiology, modes of transmission, and prevention of HBV and HIV
   2. Risks to the fetus from HBV and HIV
   3. Location and proper use of all protective equipment
   4. Proper work practices using Universal Precautions
   5. Meaning of color codes, biohazard symbol, and precautions to following handling infectious waste
   6. Procedures to follow if needlestick or other injury occurs

C. Management of an Exposure Incident:
   1. Document routes of exposure
   2. Document source
   3. Request blood screening of source

4. Advise employee to be tested
5. Provide prophylaxis treatment
6. Provide appropriate counseling
7. Evaluate post incident illness

5.05 Universal Precaution

A. Define universal precautions:
   1. The same infection control procedure for any dental procedure must be used for ALL patients. All human blood and body fluids are treated as contaminated.

B. List and explain seven appropriate personal protective guidelines:
   1. Uniform tops should be closed at the neck, disposable or easily laundered and have long sleeves with fitted cuffs. Pants and socks should cover the legs and ankles.
   2. Clinic attire must not be worn in the staff lounge or outside the dental office. Clothing must be changed daily.
   3. Hair should be worn off the shoulders and away from the face. Facial hair should be covered with a face mask or shield.
   4. Face masks must have a high bacterial infiltration efficiency rate. Masks should be changed after each patient or after becoming splattered and/or saturated.
   5. Protective eyewear should have wide side shields to protect the area around the eyes, and shatterproof lenses that are made of sturdy plastic.
   6. Gloves should be impermeable to saliva, blood, and bacteria and fit snug over the cuffs of the uniform.
   7. Other barrier items such as dental dams.

C. Describe the six guidelines for use of gloves:
   1. Gloves must be worn by all dental staff during the patient's treatment.
   2. Torn or damaged gloves must be replaced immediately.
   3. Do not wear jewelry under gloves.
   4. Change gloves frequently, with each new patient or approximately every hour.
   5. Contaminated gloves should be removed before leaving the operatory during patient treatment.
   6. Hands must be washed after glove removal and before re-gloving.

D. List three types of gloves worn:
   1. Overgloves
   2. Utility gloves
   3. Non-sterile latex or non-latex

E. List three principles of effective handwashing:
   1. Reduction of the bacterial flora on the skin
   2. Removal of surface dirt and loosened debris
   3. Provide disinfection with a long-acting antiseptic

F. List the seven steps for washing and drying of hands:
1. Remove all jewelry.
2. Wet hands with warm water.
3. Apply an ample amount of antibacterial liquid soap.
4. Vigorously rub hands together under a stream of water.
5. Rub together for a minimum of 15 seconds.
6. Rinse hands with cool water.
7. Using a paper towel, thoroughly dry your hands.

G. State three guidelines for handling contaminated laundry:
1. Protective clothing should be laundered in the office and universal precautions are followed when handling the clothing.
2. Disposable gowns are discarded daily, more often if visibly soiled.
3. Contaminated clothing that is removed from the office must be in a leak-proof bag that is labeled "Biohazard."

5.06 Management of Hazardous Materials

A. List three organizations that regulate the profession of dentistry:
1. Occupational Safety and Health Administration (OSHA)
2. Centers for Disease Control (CDC)
3. Environmental Protection Agency (EPA)

B. Define four classifications of waste:
1. General waste
2. Hazardous waste
3. Contaminated waste
4. Infectious or regulated waste

C. List four methods for disposal of waste:
1. Gloves, mask, and barriers contaminated with body fluids or blood should be discarded in impermeable plastic bags as general waste.
2. Sharps should be placed in a puncture-resistant, leakproof container and labeled as biohazard.
3. Blood, blood-soaked materials, tissue and teeth should be placed in leakproof containers, labeled biohazard and disposed of according to state guidelines for infectious waste.
4. Proper disposal of liquid chemicals or solid chemicals may vary with local and state waste management agencies. Check with the local agencies in your area.

D. Explain the five parts of the OSHA hazard communication standard:
1. Written
2. Chemical inventory
3. MSDS sheets
4. Container labeling
5. Employee training

E. General protection against chemical hazards:
   1. Hand and eye protection
   2. Ventilation
   3. Handling and storage
   4. Disposal

5.07 Cleaning/Pre-cleaning

A. Define cleaning/pre-cleaning:
   1. Initial removal of debris and reduction of bioburden

B. List three appropriate methods for cleaning instruments prior to sterilization:
   1. Ultrasonic cleaning
   2. Soaking instruments in a disinfectant solution
   3. Automatic washers

C. Explain three advantages of an ultrasonic cleaner:
   1. Reduced risk to operator from contact with contaminated instruments
   2. Penetration into difficult areas of instruments where brushes cannot reach
   3. Improved effectiveness in removing debris and blood from instruments

D. List the four steps for cleaning instruments manually:
   1. Wear heavy duty gloves, mask, and protective eyewear. Dismantle instruments if parts are detachable.
   2. Use detergent and scrub instruments with a brush under running water.
   3. Brush away from the body and avoid splashing the surrounding area.
   4. Rinse instruments thoroughly and dry on paper towels.

5.08 Disinfection

A. Define disinfection:
   1. Killing or inhibiting pathogens by chemical means. Spores are not killed by disinfection.

B. Define the term disinfectant:
   1. Chemicals that are applied to inanimate objects (countertops) that cannot be sterilized.

C. State the three types of disinfectants and their biocidal activity:
   1. High Level: Inactivates all forms of bacteria, fungi, spores, and viruses.
   2. Intermediate Level: Inactivates all forms of microorganisms except spores.
   3. Low Level: Inactivates vegetative bacteria and certain viruses, but does not destroy spores, tubercle bacilli or non-lipid viruses.

D. List five properties of an ideal disinfectant:
   1. Broad spectrum
   2. Nontoxic
   3. Easy to use

       4. Fast acting
       5. Economical

   E. Explain the four recommended chemical disinfectants:
       1. Chlorines: Sodium hypochlorite is unstable, use distilled water to improve stability. Economical, harmful to the eyes and skin.
       2. Glutaraldehydes: Solution is activated when the two containers are mixed. Not used as a surface disinfectant, toxic fumes. Caustic to skin and eye.
       3. Iodophores: Broad spectrum antimicrobial, hard water inactivates iodophores. Widely used for surgical scrubs, liquid soaps.
       4. Combination Phenolics: Used as surface disinfectants. Broad spectrum with residual biocidal activity.

5.09 **Sterilization**

   A. Define sterilization:
       1. A process (usually by heat) by which all forms of life (including spores) are completely destroyed.

   B. Explain the four approved methods for sterilization:
       1. Moist Heat (or steam under pressure): Sterilization is achieved by the action of heat and moisture. Pressure is used to reach high temperatures.
       2. Dry Heat: Sterilization is achieved by heat conducted from the exterior surface to the interior of the object.
       3. Chemical Vapor Steam: A combination of chemicals is heated under pressure which produces a gas-sterilizing agent.
       4. Ethylene Oxide: Commonly used in hospitals. Gaseous sterilization using ethylene oxide.

   C. List two items that can be sterilized using dry heat:
       1. Metal instruments in containers
       2. Instruments that may corrode or rust if exposed to moisture

   D. Explain two advantages for using steam under pressure:
       1. All spores, microorganisms, and viruses are destroyed quickly.
       2. Economical method for sterilizing instruments.

   E. List the temperatures for dry heat, steam under pressure and chemical vapor:
       1. Dry Heat: 320°F for two hours; 340°F for one hour
       2. Steam Under Pressure: 250°F at 15 pounds of pressure for 15 minutes; 30 minutes for heavy or large loads
       3. Chemical Vapor: 260° to 270°F at 20 to 40 pounds of pressure. Minimum of 20 minutes after the desired temperature and pressure is reached.

   F. List two reasons for spore testing:
       1. To ensure proper sterilization
       2. To verify proper function of the sterilizer

G. Explain the frequency of spore testing:
   1. Weekly testing is recommended.

H. Explain heat process monitoring

5.10 Instrument Processing

A. List the seven steps for instrument processing:
   1. Transport
   2. Cleaning
   3. Packaging
   4. Sterilization
   5. Storage
   6. Delivery
   7. Quality assurance

5.11 Treatment Room

A. List six features of an optimal treatment room:
   1. Floor covering is easy to clean. No carpeting.
   2. Stools and dental chairs have a smooth surface that is easily disinfected.
   3. Water faucets should be electronic or foot-operated.
   4. Dental chairs are foot-operated.
   5. Hoses are straight and removable.
   6. Syringes and handpieces are autoclavable

B. List four objects that require barrier protection:
   1. Dental light handles
   2. Head rest and dental chair
   3. Air/water syringe
   4. Saliva ejector and HVE handles

C. Explain the classification of surface categories for inanimate objects:
   1. Critical: Penetrates soft tissue or bone. Example: Needles, dental instruments. *Sterilize or dispose.*
   2. Semi-Critical: Touch intact mucous membranes and oral fluids but does not penetrate. Example: Ultrasonic handpiece, probe. *Sterilize or high level disinfectant.*
   3. Non-Critical: Does not touch mucous membranes. *Intermediate level of disinfection.*
   4. Environmental Surfaces: No contact with patient. *Intermediate to low level disinfection.*

D. List six steps in cleaning and preparing the treatment room:
   1. Wear heavy-duty gloves and mask.
   2. Flush handpieces.
   3. Select appropriate disinfectant and prepare according to manufacturer.
   4. Clean the surfaces with gauze soaked in a precleaning/disinfectant.

5. Scrub the disinfectant over the surface.
6. Wipe with disinfectant and leave the surfaces wet for manufacturers recommended time.

5.12 Dental Unit Water Lines

A. List five features of an optimal treatment room:
 1. Use water that meets EPA standards for drinking water.
 2. Consult dental manufacturer for methods to maintain quality of water.
 3. Follow manufacturer recommendations for monitoring quality of water.
 4. After each patient discharge air/water 20-30 seconds.
 5. Follow manufacturer recommendations for maintenance schedule.

B. Methods to reduce bacterial contamination of dental unit waterlines:
 1. Flush water lines for several minutes each morning.
 2. Use self-contained water system.
 3. Use periodic or continuous chemical germicides.
 4. Use sterile water for surgery.
 5. Purge water from surgery lines at end of day.
 6. Use microfilm cartridges.
 7. Use current techniques and technology.
 8. Follow manufacturer recommendations.

6.0 PATIENT MANAGEMENT
(I) Number of Tasks to Master = 66
(II) Intended Outcome: Given information about utilizing effective communication skills, non-verbal communication, obtaining information and managing patient behavior the student will be able to answer 85% of the questions on the didactic exam.
(III) Tasks:

6.01 Utilizing Effective Communication Skills

A. List 10 alternative terms to use in effective communication:
 1. Pull a tooth/remove a tooth
 2. Shot, needle/injection
 3. Pain, hurt/discomfort
 4. Plates, false teeth/dentures
 5. Spit/rinse your mouth
 6. Drugs/medication
 7. Filling/restoration
 8. Drill/prepare or handpiece
 9. Yeah/yes
 10. Cap/crown

B. List three rules of etiquette:
 1. Do not use nicknames or terms of endearment in an office setting.
 2. Compliment and praise.
 3. Avoid the subjects of politics, religion, gender, ethnic, and off-color jokes.

6.02 Non-Verbal Communication

A. Identify four key steps for improving telephone communications:
1. Smile.
2. Identify the office, yourself, and ask, "How may I help you?"
3. Listen and be attentive.
4. Take notes.

B. Describe seven items important to non-verbal communication:
1. Good grooming versus bad grooming.
2. Professional hair styles.
3. The use of fragrances and deodorants.
4. The appearance of hands and nails.
5. The effect of oral hygiene.
6. Professional attire.
7. Make-up.

C. Identify two effects of body language and posture:
1. Slouching
2. Crossed arms

D. List two examples of patient non-verbal cues:
1. Facial expressions
2. Body language

6.03 Greet the Patient

A. List eight items included in welcoming the patient as a guest:
1. Greet within 30 seconds.
2. Survey the reception area.
3. Sign in log.
4. Review the schedule.
5. Initiate the patient orientation.
6. Establish a relationship.
7. Use the patient's name.
8. Take notes.

B. List two areas of common courtesy and office etiquette that should be used when talking on the phone:
1. Common courtesy
2. Say please and thank you

C. Describe three steps in introductions:
1. Introduce self.
2. Identify others by name and title.
3. Maintain a schedule.

6.04 Obtaining Information

A. List two steps in obtaining information from a telephone call:
1. Record all information on chart.
2. Record information in ink and initial.

B. List two patient forms to be completed by the patient before treatment:
1. Patient registration
2. Medical/dental history

6.05 Managing Patient Behavior

A. Identify six patient rights:
1. To be treated without discrimination.
2. To be informed about treatment.
3. To be informed about fees
4. To have confidentiality.
5. To be taught how to maintain dental health.
6. To refuse treatment.

B. Describe two ways to comfort the *anxious* patient:
1. Validate feelings.
2. Accommodate patients' concerns.

C. Define the difference between *anxious* and the *phobic* patient:
1. Anxious: normal with enhanced feelings of concern.
2. Phobic: irrational fears.

D. List two methods of treating the phobic patient:
1. Behavior modification.
2. Hospital dentistry—general anesthesia.

E. List five steps to diffuse patient anger:
1. Let the patient release anger.
2. Do not second-guess.
3. Do not respond until the patient has fully vented.
4. Use the three F's: Feel, Felt, Found.
5. Avoid the urge to argue.

F. Identify four special patient management situations:
1. Elderly
2. Children
3. Pregnant
4. Mentally/physically challenged

7.0 ANATOMY
(I) Number of Tasks to Master = 80
(II) Intended Outcome: Given information about head and neck anatomy, oral anatomy, and dental anatomy, the student will be able to perform 85% of the following tasks with accuracy on the didactic examination.

(III) Tasks:

7.01 Head and Neck Anatomy

A. Locate and mark five bones or bony areas of the face and skull on the model or diagraph provided:
   1. Calvarium (frontal, parietal, occipital bones)
   2. Zygoma
   3. Maxilla
   4. Mandible
   5. Nasal bones

B. Locate seven landmarks of the skull on the diagram or model provided:
   1. External auditory meatus
   2. Nasal fossae
   3. Orbits of the eye
   4. Styloid process
   5. Mental foramen
   6. Mandibular foramen
   7. TMJ—temporal mandibular joint

C. Locate four sinuses on the model or diagram provided:
   1. Maxillary
   2. Ethmoid air cells
   3. Frontal
   4. Sphenoid

D. Locate and mark eight muscles of mastication and facial expression:
   1. Buccinator
   2. External pterygoid
   3. Internal pterygoid
   4. Masseter
   5. Mentalis
   6. Orbicularis oris
   7. Temporal
   8. Zygomatic major

E. Identify the nerves that supply the oral cavity:
   1. Maxillary
   2. Nasopalatine
   3. Anterior palatine
   4. Anterior superior alveolar
   5. Middle superior alveolar
   6. Posterior superior alveolar
   7. Buccal
   8. Mandibular
   9. Lingual
   10. Mental
   11. Incisive

7.02 Oral Anatomy

A. Locate and label 18 structures of the oral cavity:
1. Maxillary arch
2. Mandibular arch
3. Lips
4. Mucosa, buccal or labial
5. The dental alveolus
6. Gingiva, attached and free
7. Floor of the mouth
8. Hard palate
9. Soft palate
10. Tongue
11. Tonsillar pillars
12. Tonsils
13. Pharyngeal walls
14. Retromolar pad
15. Maxillary tuberosity
16. Vestibules, buccal or labial
17. Frenum
18. Teeth

B. Locate three of the main salivary glands:
1. Parotid gland
2. Sublingual gland
3. Submandibular gland

C. Locate and label three structures of the gingiva:
1. Gingival sulcus
2. Gingival papilla
3. Gingival margin

7.03 Dental Anatomy

A. Define the following six dental anatomy terms:
1. Primary dentition
2. Permanent dentition
3. Mixed dentition
4. Contact
5. Contour
6. Occlusion

B. Identify the four kinds of teeth.

C. Locate and label the three parts of a tooth:
1. Crown
2. Root
3. Neck

D. Locate and label five tissues of a tooth:
   1. Enamel
   2. Dentin
   3. Pulp
   4. Cementum
   5. Periodontal ligament

E. Locate and label the six maxillary anterior teeth:
   1. Maxillary central incisors (2)
   2. Maxillary lateral incisors (2)
   3. Maxillary canines (2)

F. Locate and identify the 10 maxillary posterior teeth:
   1. Maxillary first premolar (2)
   2. Maxillary second premolar (2)
   3. Maxillary first molar (2)
   4. Maxillary second molar (2)
   5. Maxillary third molar (2)

G. Locate and identify the six mandibular anterior teeth:
   1. Mandibular central incisors (2)
   2. Mandibular lateral incisors (2)
   3. Mandibular canine (2)

H. Locate and identify the 10 mandibular anterior teeth:
   1. Mandibular first premolar (2)
   2. Mandibular second premolar (2)
   3. Mandibular first molar (2)
   4. Mandibular second molar (2)
   5. Mandibular third molar (2)

I. Locate the six surfaces of a tooth:
   1. Mesial
   2. Occlusal
   3. Distal
   4. Buccal
   5. Lingual
   6. Facial

8.0 DENTAL EQUIPMENT
(I) Number of Tasks to Master = 50
(II) Intended Outcome: Given information about equipment identification and equipment uses, the student will be able to perform 85% of the following tasks necessary information, instruction, and equipment the student will be able to perform 85% of the following tasks with accuracy on the didactic examination.
(III) Tasks:

8.01 Equipment Identification

A. Describe five pieces of lab equipment:
1. Lathe
2. Handpiece/lab engine
3. Model trimmer
4. Vacuum adapter "The Machine"
5. Vibrator

B. Describe 12 pieces of equipment found in the treatment room:
1. Patient chair
2. Stools: Doctor and assistant (show footrest, indicate differences)
3. Treatment light
4. Cart/console
5. Handpieces (high speed/low speed)
6. High velocity evacuation (HVE)
7. Saliva ejector
8. Curing light
9. Air-water syringe
10. Rheostat/foot control
11. Computer
12. Amalgamator/triturator

C. Describe three items found in the sterile area:
1. Ultrasonic instrument cleaner
2. Cold disinfectant/sterilant container
3. Autoclaves/sterilization equipment

D. Describe five items in the radiographic area:
1. Control panel
2. Conventional or intraoral x-ray head
3. Lead apron-thyroid x-ray head
4. Automatic processor-daylight
5. Extraoral equipment

8.02 Equipment Uses

A. Give the uses of five lab equipment items:
1. Lathe: Polishes and grinds appliances.
2. Handpiece/Lab Engine: Trims and smooths smaller items outside the mouth.
3. Model Trimmer: Trims plaster and stone models.
4. Vacuum Adapter: Heats and adapts a variety of plastics to models, i.e., bleaching trays, mouth guards.
5. Vibrator: Used in pouring models to remove bubbles from mix and aid in pouring.

B. Give the uses of 12 treatment room items of equipment:
1. Patient Chair: Provides support and supine-seating for the patient.

2. Stools—Doctor Stool: Provides adjustable seating for the operator while performing dental treatment.
   Assistant Stool: Provides adjustable seating for the assistant while assisting in dental treatment.
3. Treatment Light: Provides illumination during dental treatment.
4. Cart/Console: Provides support supplies and easy access to equipment.
5. Handpieces: Rotary instruments that are used intraorally to cut and polish. (See dental instruments.)
6. High Velocity Evacuation: Assistant-controlled device that removes fluids and reduces aerosols. (Show tips.)
7. Saliva Ejector: Low volume device for removal oral fluids. (Show tips.)
8. Curing Light: Sets selected acrylic materials.
9. Air/Water Syringe: Provides air/water spray.
10. Rheostat-foot Control: Controls the rotary handpieces.
11. Computer: Used chairside to record and transmit data.
12. Amalgamator/Triturator: Mixes amalgam filling material.

C. Give the uses for three sterile area items:
1. Ultrasonic Instrument Cleaner: Removes debris from contaminated instruments.
2. Cold Disinfectant/Sterilant Container: Liquid for non-autoclavable items.
3. Autoclaves/Sterilization Equipment: Sterilizes equipment and instruments.

D. Give the uses of five pieces of radiographic equipment:
1. Control Panel: Controls x-ray production.
2. Conventional or Intraoral X-ray Head: Produces and directs x-rays.
3. Lead Apron: Provides patient protection during radiographs.
4. Automatic Processor: Processes x-ray film.
5. Extraoral X-ray Equipment: Takes x-rays outside the mouth.

9.0 DENTAL INSTRUMENTS AND PROCEDURES
(I) Number of Tasks to Master = 121
(II) Intended Outcome: Given information about hand/rotary instruments and dental procedures, the student will be able to perform 85% of the following tasks with accuracy on the didactic examination.
(III) Tasks:

9.01 Hand Instruments

A. Define the term "Hand Instrument".

B. Describe four components of hand instruments:
1. Handle/shaft
2. Shank
3. Blade
4. Double-ended instruments

C. Describe six basic tray set-up instruments:
   1. Mouth mirror
   2. Explorer
   3. Cotton pliers
   4. Saliva ejector/high-volume evacuator
   5. 3-way syringe tip
   6. 2 x 2

D. Describe 17 restorative instruments:
   1. Excavator/Spoon excavator
   2. Discoid-cleoid carver
   3. Hollenback carver
   4. Amalgam well
   5. Amalgam carrier
   6. Amalgam condenser/plugger
   7. Plastic composite instrument
   8. Burnisher
   9. Mixing spatula
   10. Matrix band
   11. Tofflemire/matrix retainer
   12. Wedge
   13. Articulating paper
   14. Articulating paper forceps
   15. Cord packer
   16. Hand cutting instruments
   17. Decay locator

E. Describe six instruments of a rubber dam procedure:
   1. Dental dam material
   2. Dental dam frame
   3. Dental dam hole punch
   4. Dental dam clamp forceps
   5. Dental dam clamps
   6. Floss

F. Discuss five periodontal instruments:
   1. Periodontal probe
   2. Curette
   3. Slimline ultrasonic scaler
   4. Scalers
   5. Periodontal knives

G. Describe 15 endodontic instruments:
   1. Gates glidden
   2. Barbed broach
   3. Endodontic files
   4. Endodontic syringe
   5. Paper points
   6. Gutta-percha
   7. Lentulo spirals

8. Endodontic spreader
9. Endodontic explorer
10. Endodontic condenser
11. Endodontic excavator
12. Millimeter measure
13. Rubber stoppers
14. Pulp tester
15. Apex locator

H. Describe 16 oral surgery instruments:
1. Elevator
2. Forceps
3. Surgical curette
4. Rongeur
5. Bone file
6. Bard-Parker handle
7. Blade
8. Hemostat
9. Needle holder
10. Surgical scissors
11. Tissue retractors
12. Surgical aspirator
13. Sutures
14. Bite blocks/mouth prop
15. Surgical chisel and mallet
16. Surgical handpiece/burs

9.02 Rotary Instruments

A. Describe five uses of rotary instruments:
1. Cavity preparations
2. Removing defective restorations
3. Crown preparations
4. Polishing teeth
5. Polishing and finishing restorations

B. Describe three parts of a dental bur:
1. Shank
2. Neck
3. Head

C. Identify three types of dental burs:
1. Carbide
2. Diamond stones
3. Steel burs

D. Discuss eight sizes and shapes of bur heads:
1. Round
2. Inverted cone
3. Fissures

4. Points
5. Stones
6. Mandrel
7. Rubber wheel
8. Rubber cup

E. Describe four styles of dental handpieces:
1. High-speed
2. Straight low-speed
   a. Contra-angle
   b. Prophy-angle

F. Discuss handpiece placement and removal.

G. Describe dental handpiece maintenance.

H. Discuss dental handpiece sterilization techniques.

9.03 Dental Procedures

A. List eight common dental procedures:
1. Exam
2. Prophylaxis, non-surgical periodontal therapy
3. Amalgam
4. Composite
5. Simple extraction
6. Endodontic
7. Crown and bridge preparation
8. Crown and bridge cementation

B. List tray armamentarium (tray setup):
1. Exam
2. Prophylaxis, non-surgical periodontal therapy
3. Amalgam restorations
4. Composite restorations
5. Extractions
6. Surgical procedures
7. Dental dam
8. Endodontic therapy
9. Crown and bridge preparation
10. Crown and bridge cementation
11. Anesthetics
12. Bleaching
13. Desensitization of the teeth
14. Removable prosthodontics
15. Preventive procedures
16. Impressions
17. Orthodontics
18. Occlusal adjustments

10.0 CLINICAL RECORDS

(I) Number of Tasks to Master = 84
(II) Intended Outcome: Given information about medical/dental histories, recording dental treatment, and dental/radiographic chartings, the student will be able to perform 85% of the following tasks on the didactic examination.
(III) Tasks:

10.01 Medical History

A. List six purposes for obtaining a medical history from every patient:
1. Provides information relevant to the etiology and diagnosis of oral conditions.
2. Used in treatment planning.
3. Reveals conditions, diseases, and drug therapy or reactions that may change treatment.
4. Provides insight into the emotional and/or psychological factors and attitudes that may affect patient care.
5. Provides baseline documentation for comparison at future appointments.
6. Provides a basis for legal evidence should treatment ever be called into question.

B. Describe six conditions that may limit the ability of dental personnel together required information when answering questions:
1. Some patients either cannot, or choose not, to provide correct information when answering questions.
2. Language barriers or comprehension may limit the information obtained.
3. If there is a lack of privacy where the information is requested, the patient may be less than honest.
4. If the patient does not see the relevance between certain diseases or conditions and dental treatment, information may be withheld.
5. Medical conditions may be embarrassing to report.
6. The patient may be fearful of having dental treatment refused.

C. List five factors that must be explained to the patient:
1. The need for obtaining and keeping an up-to-date medical history.
2. Assurance that the information obtained will be kept in strict confidence.
3. The relationship between general health and oral health.
4. The relationship between medical health and dental care.
5. The importance of following instructions on pre-medications, preventive dental care, and regular medical and dental care.

D. List the five components of the medical history that must be verified:
1. Recordings must be made in ink.
2. Accuracy of all dates.
3. Confirm all information.
4. Medical alert codes.
5. Patient signature verifying accuracy of all information.

10.02 Dental History

A. List eight components of the dental history required:
1. Any immediate problem, discomfort, or pair reported by the patient.
2. Information about previous restorative, preventive, and specialty dental care.
3. Attitudes regarding oral health.
4. Information about personal daily oral care.
5. Anesthetic history.
6. Medical and dental radiation history and current medications.
7. History of oral or facial injuries, past medical and dental procedures.
8. Oral habits.

10.03 Dental Charting and the Dental Exam

A. List the five parts of the dental exam:
1. Radiographs
2. Diagnostic models
3. Oral examination
4. Periodontal examination
5. Examination of the teeth

B. State six purposes of the dental charting:
1. Provides a graphic representation of existing conditions.
2. An assessment tool used to develop a patient treatment plan.
3. Used during treatment to guide procedures performed.
4. Evaluate treatment by comparing initial data with follow-up findings.
5. Provides realistic evidence for legal documentation.
6. Used in forensic investigations and/or identification.

C. Define Black's classification of cavities:
1. Class I
2. Class II
3. Class III
4. Class IV
5. Class V
5. Class VI

D. Describe two types of tooth diagrams.
1. Anatomical
2. Geometric

E. Describe the Universal numbering system for teeth:
1. Universal
2. Palmer
3. FDI/ISO

F. Chart seven dental conditions that are evaluated clinically by the dentist or dental hygienist and recorded on the dental chart:
1. Missing teeth
2. Teeth indicated for extraction
3. Occlusal caries
4. Malpositioned teeth
5. Existing restorations (amalgam, composite, gold)
6. Sealants
7. Appliances

G. Chart 11 dental conditions to be charted from radiographs:
1. Missing teeth
2. Unerupted teeth
3. Impacted teeth
4. Endodontic restorations
5. Periapical abscesses
6. Retained primary teeth
7. Retained root tips
8. Proximal carious lesions
9. Recurrent carious lesions
10. Bone loss
11. Other deviations from normal

H. State six tooth surfaces where periodontal pocket readings are recorded on the periodontal chart:
1. Distofacial
2. Facial
3. Mesiofacial
4. Distolingual
5. Lingual
6. Mesiolingual

10.04 Recording Dental Treatment

A. Record all pertinent information:
1. Record in ink
2. One entry per line
3. Anesthetic used
4. Tooth treated
5. Types of materials used
6. Clear and concise
7. Sign/Initial and date
8. Proper correction methods

11.0 ORAL PATHOLOGY
(I) Number of Tasks to Master = 68
(II) Intended Outcome: Given information about dental caries; attrition, abrasion, and soft tissue pathology, the student will be able to perform 85% of the following tasks with accuracy on the didactic examination.
(III) Tasks:

11.01 Dental Caries

A. Define caries:
   1. An abnormal condition of a tooth or bone characterized by decay, disintegration and destruction of the structure.

B. Identify the primary cause of caries:
   1. Bacterial plaque (Streptococcus mutans).

C. List four contributing factors of caries:
   1. Diet
   2. Oral hygiene
   3. Immune system
   4. Personal habits

D. Identify stages of caries development:
   1. Demineralization
   2. Caries
      a. Rampant
      b. Recurrent
      c. Root caries

E. List four subcomponents of personal habits that are contributing factors of caries:
   1. Tobacco
   2. Alcohol
   3. Sugared soda drinks
   4. Gum/candy

F. List five common locations for caries:
   1. Pit and fissures
   2. Smooth surface
   3. Interproximal
   4. Root surface/cervical

11.02 Periodontal Disease

A. Define or list the periodontal diseases:
   1. Gingivitis
   2. Periodontitis

B. Sign and Symptoms:
   1. Red, swollen or tender gingival
   2. Bleeding gingiva
   3. Loose teeth
   4. Pain or pressure when chewing
   5. Pus

C. Define necrotizing ulcerative periodontitis:

D. Define periodontal pocket:
   1. The disease process causes the normal gingival sulcus to become deeper than normal forming a pocket.

11.03 Attrition, Abrasion, and Erosion

A. Define attrition:
   1. The normal wearing away of tooth structure.

B. Identify the primary cause of accelerated attrition:
   1. Parafunctional habits

C. Identify two parafunctional habits:
   1. Clenching/bruxism
   2. Fibrous foods/chewing tobacco

D. List three contributing factors of attrition:
   1. Abrasive dentifrice
   2. Work environment
   3. Ice chewing

E. Define abrasion:
   1. The abnormal wearing away of tooth structure.

F. List the main cause of abrasion:
   1. Repetitive mechanical habits (i.e., improper toothbrushing).

G. Identify the primary cause of erosion:
   1. Repetitive and prolonged acid contact.

H. List two situations where acid is in prolonged contact with teeth:
   1. Bulimia
   2. Citrus habits

11.04 Soft Tissue Pathology

A. Describe four conditions of the tongue:
   1. Black hairy tongue
   2. Geographic tongue
   3. Fissured tongue
   4. Glossitis

B. Describe five white lesions of the mouth:
   1. Candidiasis (thrush)
   2. Benign hyperkeratosis (leukoplakia or white patches)
   3. Stomatitis nicotina (irritation from smoking)
   4. Chemical burn (aspirin burns)
   5. Trauma

C. Describe three oral lesions of the mouth:
1. Secondary herpetic lesion (cold sore)
2. Aphthous ulcer (canker sore)
3. Mucocele

D. Define seven conditions of the mouth:
1. Torus (exostosis)
2. Irritation fibroma
3. Dry mouth
4. Cyst
5. Papilloma
6. Abscess
7. Cheilitis

E. Define seven abnormalities (developmental) of the mouth:
1. Cleft palate/lip
2. Super numerary
3. Enamel dysplasia
4. Ankyloglossia
5. Macro/Micro dontia
6. Anelogenesis imperfecta
7. Arkylos tooth/impaction

F. Other:
1. Piercings
2. Drug abuse

12.0 EMERGENCY CARE
(I) Number of Tasks to Master = 60
(II) Intended Outcome: Given information about medical and dental emergency care the student will be able to perform 85% of the following tasks on the didactic examination.
(III) Tasks:

12.01 Medical Emergency Care

A. List four vital signs:
1. Temperature
2. Blood pressure
3. Pulse
4. Respiration

B. List four aspects associated with blood pressure:
1. Normal range for blood pressure (90-140/60-90).
2. Recommended technique for obtaining blood pressure.
3. Systolic and diastolic.
4. Health risks associated with high or low blood pressure and its relation to dentistry.

C. List two aspects of heart rate (pulse) and rhythm:
   1. Normal range for adult (60-100).
   2. Methods for obtaining a reading.

D. List three aspects of respiratory rate:
   1. Normal range for adult (12-20).
   2. Methods for obtaining a reading.
   3. Hyperventilation.

E. List two methods of measuring temperature:
   1. Oral
   2. Tympanic

F. Describe five ways to prevent emergencies:
   1. Obtain current and complete medical/dental history.
   2. All dental personnel competent in CPR, Heimlich maneuver, and obtaining vital signs.
   3. Assess patient during treatment.
   4. Have an office emergency plan.
   5. Have emergency equipment ready.

G. Describe the four parts of an emergency preparedness plan:
   1. Assigned roles
   2. Routine drills
   3. Emergency telephone numbers
   4. Emergency supplies

H. List four signs of an impending emergency:
   1. Change in patient breathing.
   2. Change in patent level of consciousness.
   3. Change in patient skin color.
   4. Change in patient skin temperature.

I. Describe the ABC's of CPR:
   1. A = Airway
   2. B = Breathing
   3. C = Circulation

J. List three signs that indicate it may be necessary to perform the abdominal thrust:
   1. The victim clearly indicates they are choking.
   2. The victim cannot cough.
   3. The victim cannot breathe.

12.02 Medically Compromised Patient

A. Recognize medical conditions that may compromise dental treatment.

B. Identify medications that might affect patient's dental treatment.

C. Recognize the signs and symptoms related to specific medical conditions and emergencies.

12.03 Medical Emergencies

A. Discuss emergency care standards:
1. Allergic.
2. Blood loss.
3. Cardiovascular or cerebrovascular irregularities.
4. Emergencies procedures by metabolic neurologic disease.
5. Respiratory irregularities, obstructions.
6. Shock.
7. Transient unconsciousness.

B. Recognize the signs and symptoms for specific medical emergencies.

C. Explain emergency equipment and supplies.

D. Explain emergency responses.

E. Record documentation of emergency.

12.04 Dental Emergency Care

A. List three steps in responding to an avulsed tooth that will assist in replantation:
1. If tooth is dirty, rinse with tap water. Do not scrub.
2. Gently tease tooth back into socket.
3. Patient to hold in socket while going to dental office.

B. List two steps in responding to an avulsed tooth when replantation is not possible:
1. Place tooth in milk or saline, or place in patient's cheek or a wet towel.
2. Transport to dental office as soon as possible.

C. List three situations when a patient has a fractured tooth and must be treated in a dental office as soon as possible:
1. When there is blood present which appears to be coming from the tooth or immediately around the tooth.
2. When the tooth is subluxed or displaced.
3. When you are unable to calm the patient.

D. List four recommendations for patients experiencing minor dental pain:
1. Take over-the-counter analgesic.
2. Place oil of clove for open cavity.
3. Alternate ice/heat packs 15 minutes on 15 minutes.
4. Rinse with warm salt water for soft tissue.

13.0 DENTAL ANESTHESIA

(I) Number of Tasks to Master = 75

(II) Intended Outcome: Given information about dental anesthesia and dental anesthesia terminology, the student will be able to perform 85% of the following tasks with accuracy on the didactic examination.

(III) Tasks:

13.01 Dental Anesthesia Terminology

A. Define the following 16 terms as they apply to dental anesthetic:
1. Anesthetic: A drug that causes a temporary loss of pain and sensation all or in part.
2. Analgesic: A drug that relieves pain.
3. Medical History: A collection of data provided by the patient about his/her general health.
4. Contraindication: A condition rendering some particular line of treatment not indicated or not advisable.
5. Epinephrine: A common vasoconstrictor used in local anesthetic, also called adrenaline.
6. Infiltration Anesthetic: The passage local of anesthetic fluid into tissue spaces to prevent pain.
7. Block Anesthetic: Local anesthetic injected near a main nerve trunk that prevents any pain sensation from passing from the site to the brain.
8. Topical Anesthetic: A drug applied topically to oral mucous membrane to numb the area prior to the local anesthetic injection.
9. Local Anesthetic: A drug injected into tissue to block sensation in a particular area.
10. Nitrous Oxide: An anesthetic gas used as an analgesic in dentistry; also known as laughing gas.
11. Dental Syringe: A metal or plastic container with a plunger and needle used for injections of anesthetic into the oral cavity.
12. Needle Gauge: The diameter of a needle; the needles used in dentistry are usually sizes 27 and 30.
13. Lumen: The passageway inside a hollow needle or organ.
14. Diffusion: To spread from an area of high concentration to one of low concentration.
15. Vasoconstrictor: Drugs that constrict blood vessels around the injection site.
16. Anaphylaxis: A sudden, severe, and sometimes fatal allergic reaction by an individual to specific allergens.

13.02 Dental Anesthesia

A. List and define the four most commonly used application methods of anesthetics in the dental office:
1. Topical
2. Local
3. Nitrous oxide
4. Sedation

B. Explain the four important reasons for checking a patient's medical history as it relates to dental anesthetics:
   1. A medical history informs the dental staff of a patient's physical condition.
   2. Chronic conditions.
   3. Allergies.
   4. Medications the patient is taking.

C. Explain six health conditions that can affect anesthetic choice:
   1. Hypertension
   2. Cardiovascular disease
   3. Hyperthyroidism
   4. Liver disease
   5. Kidney disease
   6. Pregnancy

D. Identify the seven parts of an aspirating syringe:
   1. Thumb-ring
   2. Finger grip
   3. Finger bar
   4. Barrel
   5. Piston rod/plunger
   6. Harpoon
   7. Threaded hub

E. Identify the four parts of a dental anesthetic needle:
   1. Plastic housing for needle.
   2. Cartridge end of the needle.
   3. Needle hub.
   4. Injection end of the needle with bevel

F. List the two lengths and gauges of needles most commonly used in dentistry:
   1. 1"-30 gauge short (commonly used for infiltration).
   2. 1-5/8" – 27 gauge long (commonly used for block).

G. Identify the three parts of an anesthetic cartridge:
   1. Rubber stopper
   2. Glass cartridge
   3. Aluminum cap with rubber diaphragm

H. List the five items needed for giving a local anesthetic injection:
   1. Topical anesthetic ointment
   2. Sterile cotton tip applicator
   3. Sterile gauze sponges (2x2)
   4. Needle shield
   5. Sterile anesthetic syringe

I. List in order the four steps for topical anesthetic site preparation and delivery:
   1. Place a small amount of topical anesthetic on a sterile cotton tip applicator.

2. Dry the proposed site with a sterile 2x2 gauze sponge.
3. Place topical anesthetic at prepared site for approximately 2-5 minutes.
4. Remove the cotton tip applicator and discard in the designated receptacle.

J. List the seven steps in loading an anesthetic syringe without the needle:
1. Select the type of anesthetic solution as indicated by the dentist and the patient's health history.
2. Hold the syringe in one hand and use the thumb-ring to pull the plunger back for insertion of the anesthetic cartridge.
3. With the other hand, load the anesthetic cartridge into the syringe barrel opening; the stopper end goes first toward the plunger.
4. Release the thumb-ring and allow the harpoon to engage into the rubber stopper.
5. Use the other hand to apply firm pressure or gentle tapping to engage the plunger harpoon into the stopper.
6. Check to make sure the harpoon is securely engaged with the rubber stopper.
7. Gently pull back on the plunger to make sure the dentist can aspirate the anesthetic during the injection.

K. List the six steps for attaching the needle to the anesthetic syringe:
1. Break the seal on the needle and remove the protective cap from the insertion area of the needle.
2. Carefully align and screw the end of the needle into position on the syringe.
3. Position the needle so it is straight and firmly attached to the diaphragm part of the cartridge, already in the syringe.
4. Dispel a very small amount of anesthetic to confirm engagement.
5. Gently pull back on the plunger to make sure aspiration is confirmed.
6. Place the prepared syringe on the tray ready for use and out of sight of the patient.

L. List the five steps for safely passing the anesthetic syringe to the dentist:
1. Loosen the needle guard.
2. Check the needle guard for stability.
3. Place the thumb-ring over the dentist's thumb, and at the same time, rotate the syringe barrel so the glass cartridge is in full view.
4. Gently but carefully and smoothly remove the needle guard as the dentist takes the syringe.
5. Put the needle guard in the needle holder. The dentist will put the used syringe into the holder, needle first, for protection of the staff.

M. List the two necessary steps needed for recapping and discarding the anesthetic needle:
1. The dental assistant or hygienist or dentist may recap the needle only by use of a needle guard or a one-handed scoop. (This procedure is usually completed by the dentist for employee protection as required by OSHA regulations.)
2. The used anesthetic needle must be discarded in a sharps container.

14.0 CHAIRSIDE ASSISTING
(I) Number of Tasks to Master = 66
(II) Intended Outcome: Given information about dental ergonomics, principles of four-handed dentistry and maintaining a clear operating field, the student will perform 85% of the following tasks with accuracy on the didactic examination.
(I) Tasks:

14.01 Dental Ergonomics

A. Define the five classifications of motion:
   1. Class I: Movement of the fingers only, as when picking up a cotton roll.
   2. Class II: Fingers and wrist motion, as used when transferring an instrument to the operator.
   3. Class III: Fingers, wrist, and elbow motion, as when reaching for a handpiece.
   4. Class IV: Movement of the entire arm and shoulder, as when reaching into a supply tub or container.
   5. Class V: Movement of the entire torso, as when turning around to reach for equipment from a side or split delivery unit.

B. List the four zones of activity:
   1. Operator's zone
   2. Assistant's zone
   3. Transfer zone
   4. Static zone

C. Describe the activities of the above four zones:
   1. Operator's Zone: Where the operator is positioned to access the oral cavity and have the best visibility.
   2. Assistant's Zone: Where the assistant is positioned to easily assist the dentist and have access to instruments, the evacuator, and so on, on the dental cart or cart without interference.
   3. Transfer Zone: Where instruments and materials are passed and received.
   4. Static Zone: Where rear delivery systems, dental instruments, mobile cart, and equipment can be found.

D. Using the face of a clock, define each zone of activity for the right-handed dentist:
   1. Operator: 7 o'clock to 12 o'clock
   2. Static: 12 o'clock to 2 o'clock
   3. Assistant: 2 o'clock to 4 o'clock
   4. Transfer: 4 o'clock to 7 o'clock

E. Using the face of a clock, define each zone of activity for the left-handed dentist:
   1. Operator: 12 o'clock to 5 o'clock
   2. Transfer: 5 o'clock to 8 o'clock
   3. Assistant: 8 o'clock to 10 o'clock
   4. Static: 10 o'clock to 12 o'clock

F. Define the three commonly used patient positions in general dentistry:
   1. Upright Position: The back of the chair is upright at a 90° angle. This position is used for patient entry and dismissal, and while taking radiographs or impressions.
   2. Supine Position: The back of the chair is lowered back until the patient's head and knees are at the same plane. Most dental treatment takes place in the supine position.
   3. Subsupine Position: The back of the chair is lowered until the patient's head is lower than the feet. This position is only recommended in emergency situations.

G. List four criteria for positioning the operator:
   1. Back straight, feet on the floor, and thighs angled so that the knees are slightly lower than hip level.
   2. Elbows close to the sides with shoulders relaxed.
   3. Patient's oral cavity should be at elbow height.
   4. The operator should be facing forward with eyes focused downward.

H. List four criteria for positioning the dental assistant:
   1. Back straight with eye level approximately four to six inches higher than the operator.
   2. Torso centered on the stool, with the stool as close to the patient as possible.
   3. Feet positioned on the ring or platform near the base of the stool.
   4. The assistant's body is facing toward the patient's head, with hips and thighs level to the floor and parallel to the patient's shoulders.

14.02 Principles of Four-Handed Dentistry

A. Define four-handed or sit-down dentistry:
   1. The dentist and dental assistant are working together at the dental chair in an effort to provide a smooth and efficient transfer of instruments and materials during patient procedures.

B. List three benefits of four-handed dentistry:
   1. Increased patient comfort and safety.
   2. Decreased stress and fatigue for the operator and assistant.
   3. Increased production with decreased chair time.

C. List six general rules of transferring instruments:
   1. Pass with the left hand (right-handed operator).
   2. Never pass instruments over the patient's face.
   3. Avoid moving the operator's hand and eyes from the working site.
   4. Always wait for a signal from the operator before exchanging instruments.
   5. Keep the passing zone close to the face, a few inches below the chin.
   6. Pass the instrument in the position of use.

D. Define the three types of instrument grasps:
   1. Pen Grasp: The instrument is held in the same manner as a pen.

2. Palm Grasp: The instrument is held in the palm of the hand.
3. Palm-Thumb Grasp: The instrument is held in the palm of the hand and the thumb is used to stabilize the instrument.

E. Define the two most commonly used types of instrument transfers:
1. One-handed Transfer: The assistant passes and receives the instrument with one hand allowing for the use of the evacuator or the air-water syringe at the same time.
2. Two-handed Transfer: The assistant uses both hands for the transfer, one to ass and the other to receive.

14.03 Maintaining a Clear Operating Field

A. List six responsibilities the dental assistant has in maintaining a clear operating field:
1. Adjust the dental light so the light shines directly on the area where the operator is working.
2. Use retraction techniques to keep tissues out of the operator's way.
3. Use evacuator to remove water, saliva, and debris from the patient's mouth.
4. Keep the operator's mirror clear during treatment.
5. Rinse and dry the area where the operator is working.
6. Help keep the patient's mouth open during the treatment.

B. List two evacuation methods:
1. Saliva ejector
2. High-volume evacuator (HVE)

C. List three isolation techniques:
1. Cotton rolls
2. Dry-angles and other related aids
3. Dental (rubber) dam

D. List two grasps that an oral evacuator may be held in:
1. Palm-thumb grasp
2. Pen grasp

E. List six guidelines for oral evacuation tip placement:
1. Hold in right hand for right-handed operator.
2. Carefully place the evacuator tip in the patient's mouth; avoid bumping the teeth, lips, or gingiva.
3. Place the evacuator tip approximately one tooth distal to the tooth being worked on.
4. Hold the bevel of the evacuator tip parallel to the buccal or lingual surface of the tooth.
5. The middle of the evacuator tip opening should be even with the occlusal surface and held still so that it does not draw the water coolant away from the bur.
6. Keep the evacuator tip far enough away from the mucosal tissue to prevent it from being sucked into the tip.

15.0 DENTAL MATERIALS

(I) Number of Tasks to Master = 82
(II) Intended Outcome: Given information about the properties and different classifications of dental materials, the student will be able to perform 85% of the following tasks with accuracy on the didactic examination.
(III) Tasks:

15.01 Properties and Classifications of Dental Materials

A. List the four properties a dental material must display to be used successfully to restore oral structures:
   1. Durability
   2. Corrosion resistance
   3. Non-toxicity
   4. Bio-compatibility

B. List and define the three properties of dental materials listed below which are evaluated to determine the materials suitability for use in the mouth:
   1. Stress: The force (per unit body) within a body that resists an external force.
   2. Strain: The distortion within a body that results from an applied force.
   3. Strength: The maximum stress required to fracture a structure.

C. Define restorative dentistry.

D. List six classifications of dental materials:
   1. Metals
   2. Resins
   3. Impression materials
   4. Gypsums
   5. Cements and liners
   6. Porcelain and ceramics

15.02 Metals in Dentistry

A. List four uses of metals in dentistry:
   1. Crowns and bridge restorations
   2. Partial dentures
   3. Implants
   4. Amalgam restorations

B. Explain six important information points about amalgam:
   1. Amalgam is the most common and widely used dental restorative worldwide.
   2. The American Dental Association and various independent agencies have studied the mercury in amalgam and reported no adverse effects.
   3. Mercury is needed to make the material into a paste form, which allows it to be placed into the tooth preparation.
   4. The mercury is lost during condensation into the tooth and over the life of the restoration as mercury vapor. (Use no touch technique.)

5. Amalgam breaks down by corrosion over time requiring replacement.
6. Amalgam is an unusual alloy composed of silver, tin, copper, and mercury.

15.03 Resins in Dentistry

A. Explain how to prepare, mix, deliver, and store dental resins:
   1. Acrylic Resins: Primarily used for denture bases and provisional (temporary) crown and bridge restoration.
   2. Composite Resins: Primarily used for restorations and cements.
   3. Glass Ionomers: Used as cements, liners, bases, and restorations.
   4. Compomers: A combination of glass ionomer and composite that is used primarily as a restorative, particularly for pediatric dentistry, because it inherently releases fluoride to the tooth structure once it is placed.

B. List the two types of bonds that occur in the resin-to-tooth bond:
   1. Mechanical
   2. Chemical

C. Explain why phosphoric acid is used to etch the surface of the enamel and dentin.
   1. This creates micro-crevasses that the liquid of the bonding agent enters into. When the bonding agent is set, it becomes a tiny finger that grabs onto microporosities and fissures in the tooth surface.

D. Explain when the chemical bond occurs:
   1. When the etchant breaks down the enamel land dentin exposing the organic component of the structure. These are primarily collagen fibers. The bonding agent has a chemical affinity to collagen, so it attaches to it.

15.04 Impression Materials in Dentistry

A. Explain how to prepare, mix, and deliver three major types of impression materials:
   1. Wax
   2. Hydrocolloid
   3. Elastomer

B. Explain the purpose of was as an impression material:
   1. To take bite registrations.

C. List two forms of hydrocolloid impression material and state their use:
   1. Reversible: Crown and bridge impressions.
   2. Irreversible (alginate): Study model impressions.

D. List the four forms of elastomeric impression materials:
   1. Polysulfide
   2. Polyether

3. Addition reaction silicone (polyvinyl siloxane or vinyl polysiloxane)
4. Condensation reaction silicone

E. Explain what "addition reaction silicone" is:
1. Used in a putty wash technique.
2. The most commonly used elastomeric impression material.

15.05 Gypsums Materials in Dentistry

A. Regarding gypsum-based materials (plaster), explain what will happen if the water-to-powder ratio varies from optimum:
1. The plaster will weaken.

B. Explain how to prepare, mix, deliver, and store gypsum products (plasters) according to ADA Spec #, Traditional Name, and Traditional Color.

ADA Spec #	Traditional Name	Traditional Color
Type I	Impression Plaster	Variable
Type II	Lab. or Model Plaster	White
Type III	Class I Dental Stone	Yellow
Type IV	Class II Dental Stone or Improved Stone	Green, Blue, or Pink

15.06 Cements and Liners in Dentistry

A. Describe three liners:
1. Calcium hydroxide
2. Cavity varnish
3. Fluoride varnish/sealants

B. Describe three uses of cements:
1. Luting
2. Temporary fillings
3. Base fillings

C. Explain how to prepare, mix, deliver, and store dental cements:
1. Glass ionomer
2. Zinc phosphate
3. Polycarboxylate
4. Zinc oxide eugenol
5. Composite resin

D. List five considerations when mixing cements:
1. Read and follow manufacturer directions.
2. Measure carefully.
3. Avoid moisture contamination.
4. Mix powder into liquid
5. Allow to set completely or according to directions.

15.07 **Porcelain and Ceramics in Dentistry**

  A. List the five major uses of porcelain in the dental office:
  1. Porcelain is used as a coating of porcelain fused to metal crowns.
  2. Porcelain is used as a crown material that can be bonded directly to the tooth.
  3. Porcelain is used as an inlay/onlay material that can be bonded directly into the tooth.
  4. Porcelain is used as teeth in dentures.
  5. Porcelain is often used as a veneering material that can be bonded to tooth structure directly.

15.08 **Other Dental Materials**

  A. Explain how to prepare, mix, deliver, and store the following:
  1. Sedative dressings
  2. Peridontal surgical dressings
  3. Post surgical dressings
  4. Bleaching agents
  5. Bonding agents
  6. Endodontic materials
  7. Etchants
  8. Pit and fissure sealants

15.09 **Lab Procedures**

  A. Describe the following laboratory procedures:
  1. Fabricate diagnostic casts.
  2. Trimming diagnostic cast.
  3. Debride and polish fixed and removable appliances and prosthesis.
  4. Splints.
  5. Fabricate custom impression trays, mouth/athletic guards, bleaching trays, acrylic temps, etc.

16.0 **INTRODUCTION TO DENTAL RADIOGRAPHY**
  (I) Number of Tasks to Master = 190
  (II) Intended Outcome: Given information about biological effects of ionizing radiation, health protection techniques, x-ray machines, dental film/sensors, radiographic landmarks, mounting radiographs and processing procedures, the student will be able to perform 85% of the following tasks with accuracy on the didactic examination.
  (III) Tasks:

16.01 **Biological Effects of Ionizing Radiation**

  A. List four tissues/cells that are highly sensitive to radiation:
  1. Bone marrow
  2. Reproductive cells
  3. Intestines
  4. Lymphoid tissue

B. List ten tissues/cells that are moderately sensitive to radiation:
   1. Oral mucosa
   2. Skin
   3. Growing bone
   4. Growing cartilage
   5. Small vasculature
   6. Connective tissue
   7. Salivary glands
   8. Mature bone
   9. Mature cartilage
   10. Thyroid gland tissue

C. List six tissues/cells that have low sensitivity to radiation:
   1. Liver
   2. Optic lens
   3. Kidneys
   4. Muscle
   5. Nerve
   6. Brain

16.02 Health Protection Techniques

A. List three methods of operator protection from primary radiation:
   1. Stand behind a protective barrier.
   2. Avoid standing in the path of the direct beam of radiation.
   3. Never hold the film for the patient during an exposure.

B. List three methods of operator protection from radiation leakage from suspected x-ray machine malfunction:
   1. Do not hold the tube housing or the Position Indicating Device (PID) during an exposure.
   2. Have the machine tested every two years.
   3. Wear a monitoring device or use area monitors to test for unwanted exposure.

C. List three methods of operator protection from secondary/scattered radiation:
   1. Stand behind the patient at a point between 90° and 135° from the source of the beam.
   2. Stand behind a wall or radiation-resistant barrier, or at least six feet away from the radiation source.
   3. Use of radiation monitoring devices—film badges or dosimeters.

D. List the six methods of radiation protection for the patient:
   1. Use the fastest film speed available—E-speed.
   2. Use open-ended, shielded, Position Indicating Devices no larger than 2.75 inches in diameter—rectangular devices are superior.
   3. Use good technique to diminish the need for retaking films.
   4. Carefully follow manufacturer's directions for processing.
   5. Use lead aprons and thyroid collars to cover the patient.
   6. ALARA (as low as reasonably achievable).

16.03 The X-ray Machine

   A. List the five major components of the x-ray machine:
      1. Tube
      2. Glass housing
      3. Tubehead
      4. Position Indicating Device (cone)
         a. Collimation
         b. Filtration
      5. Control panel adjustments

   B. Describe the five major components of the x-ray machine:
      1. Tube: Contains negative (cathode) and the positive (anode) terminals that first create, then attract electrons to produce x-rays.
      2. Glass Housing: Leaded glass that surrounds the tube.
      3. Tubehead: Heavy metal enclosure that surrounds the x-ray tube.
      4. Position Indicating Device (cone): Used to direct and contain the beam of radiation.
      5. Control panel adjustments.

16.04 Dental Film/Sensors

   A. List four types of dental films:
      1. Intraoral
         a. Film sizes
      2. Extraoral
         a. Film sizes
      3. Duplicating
      4. Digital
         a. Charge-coupled device (CCD)
         b. Complementary metal oxidesemiconductor/active pixel sensor (CMOS/APS)
         c. Charge injection device (CID)

   B. Describe film selection and uses:
      1. Perical
      2. Bitewing
      3. Occlusal
      4. Panoramic
      5. Other extraoral

   C. List three factors to consider when storing dental film:
      1. Temperature
      2. Humidity
      3. Radiation

   D. Explain the three important film storage factors:
      1. Optimum temperature for storage should be between 50° and 70° Fahrenheit.
      2. The relative humidity for film storage should be between 30% and 50%.

3. Film should be stored in areas where radiation exposures are made.

E. List three factors to consider relevant to inventory control of dental film:
1. Shelf-life
2. Numbering system
3. Packaging

F. Explain the three inventory control factors:
1. Examine the manufacturer's expiration date on film boxes and store so the oldest film is used first.
2. Store film according to size—number 0 smallest, to number 4, largest (0, 1, 2 most common).
3. Store film by package type—single film packets or double film packets.

G. Explain film composition:
1. Latent image
2. Film base
3. Adhesive layer
4. Gelatin

16.05 Radiographic Techniques

A. Paralleling Technique:
1. Advantages and disadvantages
2. Accessories used
3. Film size and type required

B. Bisecting angle technique:
1. Advantages and disadvantages
2. Accessories used
3. Film size and type required

C. Extra oral film:
1. Advantages and disadvantages
2. Accessories used
3. Film size and type required

16.06 Radiographic Infection Control

A. Define two image characteristics used to identify landmarks visible in radiographic films.
1. Radiopaque
2. Radiolucent

16.07 Patient Management for Radiography

A. Use appropriate patient management techniques before, during, and after exposure:
1. Patient concerns
2. Special needs patients

16.08 Radiographic Landmarks

A. Define five image characteristics used to identify landmarks visible in radiographic films:
1. Radiopaque
2. Radiolucent
3. Density
4. Contrast
5. Sharpness

B. Identify six landmarks visible in the maxillary molar film:
1. Maxillary sinus
2. Zygomatic process
3. Zygomatic bone
4. Hamulus
5. Maxillary tuberosity
6. Coronoid process of the mandible

C. Identify one landmark visible in the maxillary premolar film:
1. Maxillary sinus

D. Identify two landmarks visible in the maxillary canine film:
1. Maxillary sinus
2. Junction of the maxillary sinus and nasal fossa

E. Identify five landmarks visible in the maxillary incisor film:
1. Incisive foramen
2. Nasal septum
3. Nasal fossa
4. Anterior nasal spine
5. Median palatine suture

F. Identify four landmarks visible in the mandibular molar film:
1. Mandibular canal
2. Internal oblique line
3. External oblique ridge
4. Mylohyoid ridge

G. Identify one landmark visible in the mandibular premolar film:
1. Mental foramen

H. Identify three landmarks visible in the mandibular incisor film:
1. Lingual foramen
2. Mental ridge
3. Genial tubercles

16.09 Mounting Radiographs

A. Describe the eight-step procedure for mounting a full mouth set of radiographs:
1. Mark the mount with the patient name, age, date.
2. Place a clean, dry paper towel on the countertop in front of a lighted viewbox.
3. With clean, dry hands, handle radiographs by edges only.
4. Place all radiographs on the paper towel with the embossed (raised) dot facing up.
5. Sort the radiographs into three groups: bitewings, posterior periapicals, and anterior periapicals.
6. Further arrange the radiographs by maxillary arch: Posterior and anterior, and mandibular arch: posterior and anterior.
7. Separate all films left from right and orient periapical films with maxillary roots pointing up and mandibular roots pointing down.
8. Begin mounting by inserting the bitewing radiographs into the mount, followed by the posterior periapicals and finally the anterior periapicals.

16.10 Processing Procedures

A. Describe the six steps required during film processing to assure proper infection control:
1. Wipe saliva from films.
2. Place films in a labeled disposable container.
3. Wash hands.
4. With non-powdered gloved hands, and in safelight conditions, open the film packets by pulling on their tabs.
5. Allow films to drop onto a clean paper towel or into a paper cup.
6. Remove contaminated gloves, rewash hands, and re-glove prior to processing. NOTE: An alternative is to wear over gloves when opening film packets.

B. State the ten steps required to hand process films:
1. Check solution levels.
2. Maintain appropriate chemical temperatures: between 68° and 70°.
3. Turn white lights off and safelight on.
4. Using appropriate methods of infection control, remove films from packets.
5. Securely place films onto hanger.
6. Immerse film in developer and activate timer for five minutes.
7. Remove from developer and rinse by agitation for 30 seconds.
8. Immerse films in fixer and activate timer for 10 minutes.
9. Remove films and place in circulating water bath for 10 minutes.
10. Dry films in electric dryer or air-dry until films are no longer tacky.

C. State four principles of operation for automatic processing:
1. Manufacturer's recommendations must be followed precisely.
2. Rollers or tracks are used to transport the films through the processing chemicals.

3. Much higher temperatures are required for automatic processing.
4. Chemical concentrations are higher for automatic processing.

D. Describe three elements of caring for the automatic processor:
1. Special cleaning films must be run through the system daily.
2. Depending on usage, the processor must be scoured with a nylon pad weekly or biweekly. Harsh cleansers should not be used.
3. At the same time interval, the rollers should be removed from roller-type systems and soaked in warm water for 20 minutes, then special cleaning solutions used.

E. Describe the three principles for care of processing solutions:
1. Levels of the solutions must be checked regularly and replenished as required by manufacturer recommendation.
2. If large films such as panoramic films are processed frequently, the solutions will need to be replenished more often.
3. Solutions should be changed at least every four weeks.

F. Describe quality assurance procedures:
1. Recording solution temperatures.
2. Dates of solution changes.
3. Test films.
4. Equipment maintenance
5. Inspections

16.11 Evaluating Radiographs for Diagnostic Value

A. Identify interoral exposure errors and causes.
1. Elongation
2. Foreshortening
3. Horizontal overlap
4. Cone cutting
5. Light image
6. Dark image
7. Film bending
8. Reverse film (herringbone effect)
9. Black (clear) film
10. Blurred image
11. Superimposed image
12. Double exposure
13. Saliva lead
14. Film placement errors

B. Identify extraoral exposure errors and cause:
1. Patient positioning errors
2. Film placement errors

C. Identify processing errors and causes:
1. Spots on film
2. Fogging
3. Light and dark images

4. Clear (blank) film
5. Particle images
6. Stains
7. Discoloration
8. Overlapped films
9. Air bubbles
10. Scratches
11. White or black lines
12. Static electricity artifacts
13. Fingerprints

SECTION 2: CLINICAL EDUCATION: FUNDAMENTALS OF DENTAL ASSISTING

Table 2. Educational Parameters of the Clinical/Lab Component of the Fundamentals of Dental Assisting Curriculum: Procedures		
Unit	Title	Number of Tasks
1	Disclosing Procedure	5
2	Brushing Procedure	12
3	Flossing Procedure	7
4	Vital Signs Measurement Procedure	7
5	Personal Protective Equipment (PPE) Procedure	11
6	Mounting Radiographs Procedure	6
7	Acrylic Disk Polishing Procedure	7
8	Diagnostic Cast Procedure (Working with Alginate and Dental Plaster Lab)	20
9	Treatment Room Breakdown Procedure	17
	Total	92

1.0 DISCLOSING PROCEDURE
(I) Number of Tasks to Master = 5
(II) Intended Outcome: Given disclosing tablets or disclosing solution, lip lubricant, safety glasses, gloves, mask, soap, paper towels, mouth mirror, hand mirror, cotton tip applicator, cup, water, and a sink (if available), the student will perform the following tasks on a partner with 100% accuracy.
(III) Tasks:

1. Take universal precautions.

2. Apply lip lubricant on partner's lips.

3. Refer to manufacturer's instructions prior to using the disclosing solution or tablets. If using disclosing tablets, have your partner chew one table thoroughly, swish with water, and expectorate (spit) into a cup or sink. If using the disclosing solution, apply a small amount of solution on a cotton tip applicator and glide the applicator over all the surfaces of the teeth. Instruct your partner to rinse with water and expectorate into a cup or sink.

4. Using a mouth mirror, look in your partner's mouth and identify the areas of plaque on the surfaces of the teeth. Holding a hand mirror, your partner will also look in the mouth and identify the areas of plaque on tooth surfaces. (NOTE: Areas where plaque is present on the teeth will stain a color.)

5. Disinfect the surface area where you are working. Your partner will follow the same procedures (1-4).

2.0 BRUSHING PROCEDURE
(I) Number of Tasks to Master = 12
III) Intended Outcome: Given a mouth mirror and soft bristle toothbrush, the student will perform the following tasks with 100% accuracy.
(III) Tasks:

1. Grasp the toothbrush with a firm grip and utilize a hand mirror to assess tooth brushing technique.

2. Begin on the maxillary buccal surfaces of the two most posterior teeth. Angle the toothbrush at a 45° angle to the long axis of the tooth.

3. Choosing no more than two teeth at a time, gently move the toothbrush against the teeth and gums using small vibratory strokes. Brush for a count of 10.

4. Continue around the mouth until all the buccal and facial surfaces have been brushed.

5. Begin on the maxillary lingual surfaces of the two most posterior teeth and continue until all the lingual surfaces have been brushed.

6. Begin on the mandibular quadrant on the buccal surfaces of the two most posterior teeth. Angle the toothbrush at a 45° angle to the long axis of the tooth.

7. Choosing no more than two teeth at a time, gently move the toothbrush against the teeth and gums using small vibratory strokes. Brush for a count of 10.

8. Continue around the mouth until all the buccal and facial tooth surfaces have been brushed.

9. Continue on the mandibular lingual surfaces of the two most posterior teeth and continue until all the lingual surfaces have been brushed.

10. Begin on the furthermost tooth in a maxillary quadrant. Place the bristles on the chewing surface of the teeth and use a back-and-forth motion across the occlusal surfaces. Brush from the furthermost tooth toward the premolars for a count of 10.

11. Continue until all the occlusal surfaces have been brushed.

12. Rinse to remove plaque and debris

3.0 FLOSSING PROCEDURE
(I) Number of Tasks to Master = 7
(II) Intended Outcome: Using waxed or unwaxed dental floss, a hand mirror, and the assistance of a partner, the student will perform the following tasks on themselves with 100% accuracy.
(III) Tasks:

1. Your partner will hold the hand mirror while you practice. Remove a piece of floss approximately 18 inches long.

2. Wrap the ends of the floss around your middle fingers until the length of the floss is approximately two inches. Use your other fingers to help guide the floss.

3. Beginning on the most posterior interproximal surface of a mandibular or maxillary tooth, glide the floss between the teeth using a back-and-forth motion. Avoid snapping the floss against the gum tissue.

4. Curve the floss in a C-shape around the tooth. Guide the floss into the sulcus maintaining a C-shape. Gently floss the area four to five times using an up and down motion.

5. Remove the floss from the sulcus area and curve the floss in a C-shape around the opposing tooth. Glide the floss into the sulcus, maintaining a C-shape. Gently floss the area four to five times using an up and down motion.

6. Remove the floss from the contact area with an upward gliding motion. Unwrap the floss from the fingers and wrap a new section of unused floss around the same fingers. Proceed to the next interproximal area.

7. Continue in this manner until all the interproximal surfaces have been flossed.

4.0 VITAL SIGNS PROCEDURE
(I) Number of Tasks to Master = 7
(II) Intended Outcome: Given the knowledge of vital statistics, a sphygmomanometer, a stethoscope, a thermometer, a timepiece, a chart, a writing instrument, and a patient, the student will perform the following tasks with 100% accuracy.
(III) Tasks:

1. Have the patient bare an arm without obstruction up to the shoulder.

2. Place the sphygmomanometer around the upper arm between the shoulder and the elbow, with the pressure gauge tubing lined up over the medial aspect of the antecubital fossa.

3. Place the earpieces of the stethoscope in the ears and the tympanic piece over the brachial artery in the antecubital fossa.

4. Inflate the cuff until there is not a pulse sound appreciated through the stethoscope (usually 160 to 180).

5. As pressure is released from the cuff, record the pressure reading on the gauge when you first hear a pulse sound then again when the pulse sound is no longer heard.

6. Place the pads of the index and middle fingers on the inner surface of the patient's wrist (between the radius and the tendon). Start counting with 0 for the first pulse; the next pulse will be counted as 1 and so on. Count the pulse for thirty seconds and then multiply by 2 to complete the rate for one full minute.

7. Using a timepiece and watching the patient, count the number of breaths taken in a 20 second period, multiply this number by three, and then record the number.

5.0 PERSONAL PROTECTIVE EQUIPMENT PROCEDURE
(I) Number of Tasks to Master = 11
(II) Intended Outcome: Given the necessary personnel supplies (lab jacket, gloves, masks, and goggles) to don and take off personal protective equipment, the student will perform the following tasks with 100% accuracy.
(III) Tasks:

5.01 Don Personal Protective Equipment

1. Put on fresh lab jacket and fasten properly.

2. Put on protective eyewear.

3. Place mask on face and fasten properly; adjust the nose area to fit snugly.

4. Wash and dry hands, then put on exam gloves.

5. Tuck cuff of sleeves into the gloves.

5.02 Removing Personal Protective Equipment

1. Grasp the cuff of the first glove and pull it off, turning it inside out. As you do, keep this glove in the gloved hand.

2. With the ungloved hand, grasp the inside of the cuff of the other glove, pull the glove off turning it inside out, keeping the first glove inside. Throw the gloves in the proper waste receptacle.

3. Grasp the elastic or ties of the mask and remove it from the face, being cautious not to touch the contaminated front area. Throw the mask away.

4. Grasp the protective eyewear by the earpiece and remove from the face. Place by sink to clean and disinfect.

5. Remove the lab jacket and place in the proper area.

6. Wash hands.

6.0 MOUNTING RADIOGRAPHS PROCEDURE
(I) Number of Tasks to Master = 6
(II) Intended Outcome: Given the knowledge of dental anatomy, eighteen (18) developed radiographs, a mount, table surface, and a light source, the student will be able to perform the following tasks with 100% accuracy.
(III) Tasks:

1. Arrange all dental films with dimples facing up from table top.

2. Group bitewings, anterior periapicals, and posterior periapicals.

3. Separate maxillary from mandibular periapicals.

4. Separate all films left and right. (NOTE: With the dimple facing toward the reader, identify the teeth in the radiograph and place with teeth anteriorly to center of the mount.

5. Insert each film into the appropriate slot on the x-ray mount (dimple facing up).

6. Label the mounts with patient name and date.

7.0 ACRYLIC DISK POLISHING PROCEDURE
(I) Number of Tasks to Master = 7
(II) Intended Outcome: Given the necessary didactic instruction, supplies, and equipment to perform polishing acrylic, the student will perform the following tasks on an acrylic disk with imperfections with 100% accuracy.
(III) Tasks:

1. Assemble acrylic disk polishing tray set up.
   a. Gloves
   b. Eyewear
   c. Acrylic disc
   d. Lathe
   e. Arbor band or latch-type acrylic bur
   f. Slow speed handpiece
   g. Wet-rag wheel
   h. Medium grit pumice
   i. Flour of pumice

2. Take required safety precautions.

3. Reduce the bulk with the arbor band on the lathe or an acrylic bur in the handpiece.

4. Refine surface with an acrylic bur in the handpiece.

5. Polish on low with a wet-rag wheel and medium pumice.

6. Polish on low with a wet-rag wheel and flour of pumice.

7. Rinse and evaluate disk.

8.0 DIAGNOSTIC CAST PROCEDURE (WORKING WITH ALGINATE AND DENTAL PLASTER LABORATORY)
(I) Number of Tasks to Master = 20
(II) Intended Outcome: Given the necessary diagnostic casting equipment and supplies, the student will perform the following tasks with 100% accuracy.
(III) Tasks:

1. Assemble the diagnostic cast procedure tray set up.
   a. Flexible mixing bowl
   b. Large mixing spatula
   c. Small mixing spatula
   d. Vibrator
   e. Dental model plaster
   f. Rubber model base formers
   g. Maxillary stock tray to fit the typodont model
   h. Mandibular stock tray to fit the typodont model

i. Typodont model
j. Sink for water and hand washing
k. Paper towels
l. Gloves

2. Produce a diagnostic model of the dental arches by performing the following twenty tasks:
   a. Wash, dry, and glove hands.
   b. Select a tray that will fit the typodont model provided.
   c. Measure out the alginate powder.
   d. Measure out the correct amount of water.
   e. Pour the alginate into the mixing bowl.
   f. Pour the water into the mixing bowl.
   g. Mix the material until the mix is creamy, remembering to keep the amount of air incorporation to a minimum to prevent bubble formation.
   h. Load the mandibular tray.
   i. Place the loaded tray onto the mandibular teeth of the typodont in a manner that simulates insertion into an actual patient's mouth. This must be done remembering to seat the posterior section of the tray first and then rocking it onto the anterior teeth.
   j. Once the material is set, remove the impression from the typodont and repeat the procedures for the upper arch.
   k. Have the instructor check the impressions to ensure all the teeth are registered without excessive show-through on the occlusal, that the extensions of the impressions are appropriate (i.e., vestibules, palate, throat) and that all the teeth are properly registered.
   l. Proceed to pour-up the impressions by measuring the dental plaster into the flexible bowl.
   m. Measure out the correct amount of water and pour it into the mixing bowl.
   n. Mix the material with the intention of preventing a lot of air incorporation, check consistency (smooth and creamy with body) and use the vibrator to eliminate as much of the incorporated air as possible from the mix.
   o. Pour the impressions by dipping a small amount of plaster out of the mix with a mixing spatula and running the mixture into the impression from one point using the vibrator to help the material slowly advance to each of the teeth and other features of the impression.
   p. Lay the poured impression aside for a moment while a sufficient quantity of the mixed plaster is loaded into the rubber base former.
   q. Invert the poured impression over the base former and seat without embedding the tray itself in the plaster.
   r. Repeat these procedures with the other impression.
   s. Once the plaster is set (45-60 minutes), remove the impressions from the new model without breaking teeth.
   t. Have the instructor inspect the study model to determine acceptability.

9.0 TREATMENT ROOM BREAKDOWN PROCEDURE
(I) Number of Tasks to Master = 17
(II) Intended Outcome: Given the necessary didactic instruction, supplies and equipment to breakdown a dental treatment room, the student will perform the following tasks with 100% accuracy.

(III) Tasks:

1. Remove mask and gloves following completion of the dental procedure. Leave safety glasses on.

2. Complete chart entry.

3. Walk patient out to the front desk.

4. Return to treatment room.

5. Put on utility gloves.

6. Clear tray of disposables.

7. Place items into the biobag at the unit.

8. Run handpieces 30 seconds.

9. Remove handpieces and place on tray.

10. Strip barriers off of chair, stools, cart, and light.

11. Wipe handpieces, HVE, a/w syringes with disinfectant.

12. Lay handpieces, HVE, a/w syringes on a paper towel and spray them with an acceptable disinfectant.

13. Take tray of contaminated items to the sterilization area and separate.

14. Remove the barrier from the instrument tray.

15. Return to the treatment room, spray glasses with disinfectant.

16. Spray utility gloves with disinfectant.

17. Wash hands.

Table 3. Educational Parameters of the Clinical/Lab Component of the Fundamentals of Dental Assisting Curriculum: Evaluation		
Unit	Title	Number of Tasks
1	Disclosing Procedure	5
2	Brushing Procedure	12
3	Flossing Procedure	7
4	Vital Signs Procedure	7
5	Personal Protective Equipment Procedure	11
6	Mounting Radiographs Procedure	6
7	Acrylic Disk Polishing Procedure	7
8	Diagnostic Cast Procedure	20
9	Treatment Room Breakdown Procedure	17
	Total	92

FUNDAMENTALS OF DENTAL ASSISTING
COMPETENCY-BASED CLINICAL EVALUATION

1.0 DISCLOSING PROCEDURE

Student Name:_____
Lab Evaluator:_____ Date_____ Grade: [ ] Pass [ ] Fail
CL Evaluator:_____ Date_____ Grade: [ ] Pass [ ] Fail

Intended Outcome: Given disclosing tablets or disclosing solution, lip lubricant, safety glasses, gloves, mask, soap, paper towels, mouth mirror, hand mirror, cotton tip applicator, cup, water, and a sink (if available), the student will perform the following tasks on themselves and their partner with 100% accuracy.

	Tasks	Clinical/Laboratory	
		Pass	Fail
1.	Take universal precautions		
2.	Apply lip lubricant on partner's lips.		
3.	Refer to manufacturer's instruction prior to using the disclosing solution or tablets. If using tablets, have your partner chew one tablet thoroughly, swish with water and expectorate (spit) into a cup or sink. If using the disclosing solution, apply a small amount of solution on a cotton tip applicator and glide the applicator over all the surfaces of the teeth. Instruct your partner to rinse with water and expectorate into a cup or sink.		
4.	Using a mouth mirror, look in your partner's mouth and identify the areas of plaque on the surface of the teeth. Holding a hand mirror, your partner will also look in the mouth and identify areas of plaque on tooth surfaces. (Note: Areas where plaque is present on the teeth will stain a color.)		
5.	Disinfect the surface area where you are working. Your partner will follow the same procedure (Steps 1-4 above).		
Comments			

2.0 BRUSHING PROCEDURE

Student Name:_____
Lab Evaluator:_____ Date_____ Grade: [ ] Pass [ ] Fail
CL Evaluator:_____ Date_____ Grade: [ ] Pass [ ] Fail

Intended Outcome: Given a mouth mirror and soft bristle toothbrush, the student will perform the following tasks with 100% accuracy.

	Tasks	Clinical/Laboratory	
		Pass	Fail
1.	Grasp the toothbrush with a firm grip and utilize a hand mirror to assess tooth brushing technique.		
2.	Begin on the maxillary buccal surfaces of the two most posterior teeth. Angle the toothbrush at a 45° angle to the long axis of the tooth.		
3.	Choosing no more than two teeth at a time, gently move the toothbrush against the teeth and gums using small vibratory strokes. Brush for a count of 10.		
4.	Continue around the mouth until all the buccal and facial surfaces have been brushed.		
5.	Begin on the maxillary lingual surfaces of the two most posterior teeth and continue until all the lingual surfaces have been brushed.		
6.	Begin on the mandibular quadrant on the buccal surfaces of the two most posterior teeth. Angle the toothbrush at a 45° angle to the long axis of the tooth.		
7.	Choosing no more than two teeth at a time, gently move the toothbrush against the teeth and gums using small vibratory strokes. Brush for a count of 10.		
8.	Continue around the mouth until all the buccal and facial tooth surfaces have been brushed.		
9.	Continue on the mandibular lingual surfaces of the two most posterior teeth and continue until all the lingual surfaces have been brushed.		
10.	Begin on the furthermost tooth in a maxillary quadrant. Place the bristles on the chewing surface of the teeth and use a back-and-forth motion across the occlusal surfaces. Brush from the furthermost tooth toward the premolars for a count of 10.		
11.	Continue until all the occlusal surfaces have been brushed.		
12.	Rinse to remove plaque and debris.		
Comments			

3.0 FLOSSING PROCEDURE

Student Name:_____

Lab Evaluator:_____ Date_____ Grade: [ ] Pass [ ] Fail
CL Evaluator:_____ Date_____ Grade: [ ] Pass [ ] Fail

Intended Outcome: Using waxed or unwaxed dental floss, a hand mirror, and the assistance of a partner, the student will perform the following tasks on themselves with 100% accuracy.

	Tasks	Clinical/Laboratory	
		Pass	Fail
1.	Your partner will hold the hand mirror while you practice. Remove a piece of floss approximately 18 inches long.		
2.	Wrap the ends of the floss around your middle fingers until the length of the floss is approximately two inches. Use your other fingers to help guide the floss.		
3.	Beginning on the most posterior interproximal surface of a mandibular or maxillary tooth, glide the floss between the teeth using a back-and-forth motion. Avoid snapping the floss against the gum tissue.		
4.	Curve the floss in a C-shape around the tooth. Guide the floss into the sulcus maintaining a C-shape. Gently floss the area four to five times using an up and down motion.		
5.	Remove the floss from the sulcus area and curve the floss in a C-shape around the opposing tooth. Glide the floss into the sulcus, maintaining a C-shape. Gently floss the area four to five ties using an up and down motion.		
6.	Remove the floss from the contact area with an upward gliding motion. Unwrap the floss from the fingers and wrap a new section of unused floss around the same fingers. Proceed to the next interproximal area.		
7.	Continue in this manner until all the interproximal surfaces have been flossed.		
Comments			

4.0 VITAL SIGNS PROCEDURE

Student Name:_____
Lab Evaluator:_____Date_____ Grade: [ ] Pass [ ] Fail
CL Evaluator:_____Date_____ Grade: [ ] Pass [ ] Fail

Intended Outcome: Given the knowledge of vital statistics, a sphygmomanometer, a stethoscope, a thermometer, a timepiece, a chart, a writing instrument, and a patient, the student will perform the following tasks with 100% accuracy.

	Tasks	Clinical/Laboratory	
		Pass	Fail
1.	Have the patient bare an arm without obstruction up to the shoulder.		
2.	Place the sphygmomanometer around the upper arm between the shoulder and the elbow, with the pressure gauge tubing lined up over the medial aspect of the antecubital fossa.		
3.	Place the earpieces of the stethoscope in the ears and the tympanic piece over the brachial artery in the antecubital fossa.		
4.	Inflate the cuff until there is not a pulse sound appreciated through the stethoscope. (Usually 160 to 180)		
5.	As pressure is released from the cuff, record the pressure reading on the gauge for when you first hear a pulse sound then again when the pulse sound is no longer heard.		
6.	Place the pads of the index and middle fingers on the inner surface of the patient's wrist (between the radius and the tendon). Start counting with 0 for the first pulse; the next pulse felt will be counted as 1 and so on. Count the pulse for thirty seconds and then multiply by 2 to complete the rate for one full minute.		
7.	Using a timepiece and watching the patient, count the number of breaths taken in a 20 second period, multiply this number by three, and then record the number.		
Comments			

5.0 PERSONAL PROTECTIVE EQUIPMENT PROCEDURE

Student Name:_____
Lab Evaluator:_____Date_____ Grade: [ ] Pass [ ] Fail
CL Evaluator:_____Date_____ Grade: [ ] Pass [ ] Fail

Intended Outcome: Given the necessary personal supplies (lab jacket, gloves, masks, and goggles) to don and take off personal protective equipment, the student will perform the following tasks with 100% accuracy.

	Tasks	Clinical/Laboratory	
		Pass	Fail
Don Personal Protective Equipment			
1.	Put on fresh lab jacket and fasten properly		
2.	Put on protective eyewear.		
3.	Placed mask on face and fasten properly, adjust nose area to fit snugly.		
4.	Wash and dry hands, then put on exam gloves.		
5.	Tuck cuff of sleeves into the gloves.		
Removing Personal Protective Equipment			
1.	Grasp the cuff of the first glove and pull it off turning it inside out. As you do, keep this glove in the gloved hand.		
2.	With the ungloved hand, grasp the inside of the cuff of the other glove, pull the glove off turning it inside out, keeping the first glove inside. Throw the gloves in the proper waste receptacle.		
3.	Grasp the elastic or ties of the mask and remove it from the face, being cautious not to touch the contaminated front area. Throw the mask away.		
4.	Grasp the protective eyewear by the earpiece and remove from the face. Place by sink to clean and disinfect.		
5.	Remove the lab jacket and place in the proper area.		
6.	Wash hands.		
Comments			

6.0 DISCLOSING PROCEDURE

Student Name:_____
Lab Evaluator:_____Date_____ Grade: [ ] Pass [ ] Fail
CL Evaluator:_____Date_____ Grade: [ ] Pass [ ] Fail

Intended Outcome: Given the knowledge of dental anatomy, eighteen (18) developed radiographs, a mount, table surface, and a light source, the student will be able to perform the following tasks with 100% accuracy.

	Tasks	Clinical/Laboratory	
		Pass	Fail
1.	Arrange all dental films with dimples facing up from table top.		
2.	Group bitewings, anterior periapicals, and posterior periapicals.		
3.	Separate maxillary from mandibular periapicals.		
4.	Separate all films left and right. (Note: With the dimple facing toward the reader, identify the teeth in the radiograph and place with teeth anteriorly to center of the mount.		
5.	Insert each film into the appropriate slot on the x-ray mount (dimple facing up).		
6.	Label the mounts with patient name and date.		
Comments			

7.0 ACRYLIC DISK POLISHING PROCEDURE

Student Name:_____
Lab Evaluator:_____Date_____ Grade: [ ] Pass [ ] Fail
CL Evaluator:_____Date_____ Grade: [ ] Pass [ ] Fail

Intended Outcome: Given the necessary didactic instruction, supplies, and equipment to perform polishing acrylic, the student will perform the following tasks on an acrylic disk with imperfections with 100% accuracy.

	Tasks	Clinical/Laboratory	
		Pass	Fail
1.	Assemble acrylic disk polishing tray set up. Gloves Eyewear Acrylic disk Lathe Arbor band or latch-type acrylic bur Slow speed handpiece Wet-rag wheel Medium grit pumice Flour of pumice		
2.	Take required safety precautions.		
3.	Reduce the bulk with the arbor band on the lathe or an acrylic bur in the handpiece.		
4.	Refine surface with an acrylic bur in the handpiece.		
5.	Polish on low with a wet-rag wheel and medium pumice.		
6.	Polish on low with a wet-rag wheel and flour of pumice.		
7.	Rinse and evaluate disk.		
Comments			

8.0 DIAGNOSTIC CAST PROCEDURE

Student Name:_____
Lab Evaluator:_____Date_____ Grade: [ ] Pass [ ] Fail
CL Evaluator:_____Date_____ Grade: [ ] Pass [ ] Fail

Intended Outcome: Given the necessary diagnostic casting equipment and supplies, the student will perform the following tasks with 100% accuracy.

	Tasks	Clinical/Laboratory	
		Pass	Fail
Set up the workstation by assembling the following 12 materials:			
	Flexible mixing bowl		
	Large mixing spatula		
	Small mixing spatula		
	Vibrator		
	Dental model plaster		
	Rubber model base formers		
	Maxillary stock tray to fit the typodontal model		
	Mandibular stock tray to fit the typodontal model		
	Sink for water and hand washing		
	Paper towels		
	Gloves		
Produce a diagnostic model of the dental arches by performing the following 20 tasks:			
1.	Wash, dry, and glove hands.		
2.	Select a tray that will fit the typodont model provided.		
3.	Measure out the alginate powder.		
4.	Measure out the correct amount of water.		
5.	Pour the alginate into the mixing bowl.		
6.	Pour the water into the mixing bowl.		
7.	Mix the material until the mix is creamy, remembering to keep the amount of air incorporation to a minimum to prevent bubble formation.		
8.	Load the mandibular tray.		
9.	Place the loaded tray onto the mandibular teeth of the typodont in a manner that simulates insertion into an actual patient's mouth. This must be done remembering to seat the posterior section of the tray first and then rocking it onto the anterior teeth.		
10.	Once the material is set, the student will remove the impression from the typodont and repeat the procedures for the upper arch.		
11.	Have the instructor check the impressions to ensure all the teeth are registered without excessive show-through on the occlusal, that the extensions of the impressions are appropriate, and that all the teeth are properly registered.		
12.	Proceed to pour-up the impressions by measuring the		

	Tasks	Clinical/Laboratory	
		Pass	Fail
	dental plaster into the flexible bowl.		
13.	Measure out the correct amount of water and pour it into the mixing bowl.		
14.	Mix the material with the intention of preventing a lot of air incorporation and use the vibrator to eliminate as much of the incorporated air as possible from the mix. Determine correct consistency.		
15.	Pour the impressions by dipping a small amount of plaster out of the mix with a mixing spatula and running the mixture into the impression from one point using the vibrator to help the material slowly advance to each of the teeth and other features of the impression.		
16.	Lay the poured impression aside for a moment while a sufficient quantity of the mixed plaster is loaded into the rubber base former.		
17.	Invert the poured impression over the base former and seat without embedding the tray itself in the plaster.		
18.	Repeat the procedures with the other impression.		
19.	Once the plaster is set (45-60 minutes), remove the impressions from the new model without breaking teeth.		
20.	Have the instructor inspect the study model for acceptability.		
Comments			

9.0 TREATMENT ROOM BREAKDOWN PROCEDURE

Student Name:_____
Lab Evaluator:_____Date_____ Grade: [ ] Pass [ ] Fail
CL Evaluator:_____Date_____ Grade: [ ] Pass [ ] Fail

Intended Outcome: Given the necessary didactic instruction, supplies, and equipment to breakdown a dental treatment room, the student will perform the following tasks with 100% accuracy.

	Tasks	Clinical/Laboratory	
		Pass	Fail
1.	Remove mask and gloves following completion of the dental procedure. Leave safety glasses on.		
2.	Complete chart entry.		
3.	Walk patient out to the front desk.		
4.	Return to treatment room.		
5.	Put on utility gloves.		
6.	Clear tray of disposables.		
7.	Place items into the biobag at the unit.		
8.	Run handpieces for 30 seconds.		
9.	Remove handpieces and place on tray.		
10.	Strip barriers off of chair, stools, cart, and light.		
11.	Wipe handpieces, HVE, a/w syringes with disinfectant.		
12.	Lay handpieces, HVE, syringes on a paper towel and spray them with an acceptable disinfectant.		
13.	Take tray of contaminated items to the sterilization area and separate.		
14.	Remove the barrier from the instrument tray.		
15.	Return to the treatment room, remove glasses, spray with disinfectant.		
16.	Spray utility gloves with disinfectant.		
17.	Wash hands.		
Comments			

GLOSSARY

BASIC DENTAL TERMS

The dental assistant should make every effort to use correct medical and dental terminology. Following is a glossary that defines some of the terms that the dental assistant should know.

Abrasion: The wearing away of tooth structure as a result of some unusual or abnormal process, such as nervous biting habits or faulty tooth-brushing methods.

Abscess: A localized collection of pus.

Abutment: Natural tooth to which one end of a fixed or removable partial denture is attached.

Acute: Having a rapid onset, showing pronounced symptoms, and lasting a relatively short time; not chronic.

Ala: The wing of the nostril.

Allergy: Hypersensitivity to some substance.

Alloy: A mixture of two or more metals that are mutually soluble in the molten condition.

Alveolar: Pertaining to the processes of the jaws in which the roots of the teeth are embedded.

Alveolus: The cavity or socket in the alveolar process in which the roots of a tooth are held by the periodontal ligament.

Amalgam: An alloy of silver, tin, copper, and zinc mixed with mercury.

Ameloblast: Enamel-forming cell.

Ampule: A small glass container that, when sealed, holds solutions or other preparations under sterile conditions.

Analgesic: An agent used to relieve pain.

Anaphylactic Shock: A severe allergic reaction.

Anesthesia: Loss of sensation.

Anesthetic: An agent that causes anesthesia.

Anterior Teeth: Teeth located in the front of the mouth: the incisors and cuspids.

Antibiotic: A chemical substance produced by certain microorganisms that will inhibit the growth of or destroy other microorganisms.

Antidote: A remedy for counteracting the effects of a poison.

Antiseptic: An agent that prevents or arrests the growth of microorganisms without destroying them.

Antisialagogue: An agent that checks the flow of the saliva.

Apex: Tip or end of a tooth root.

Apical: Pertaining to the apex.

Apicoectomy: Cutting off the apex of a tooth root; root resection.

Aspiration: The act of breathing or drawing in; the act of removing fluids from a cavity by means of a suction device.

Attrition: The normal wearing away of the tooth surfaces.

Autoclave: An apparatus that sterilizes instruments and materials by subjecting them to steam under pressure.

Bacterial Plaque: Colorless, jelly-like deposit that clings to the surface of a tooth; it is made up primarily of bacteria, cells, and sticky substances from the saliva.

Bactericide: An agent that destroys bacteria.

Bacteriostatic: Inhibiting the growth and reproduction of bacteria.

Bacterium: Any one of a large class of microorganisms.

Bevel: A slanting edge or surface.

Blood Pressure: The force exerted by the blood against the walls of the arteries.

Bone: The hard, rigid connective tissue; the hardest substance in the body except for enamel and dentin. A part of the skeleton, such as the sternum (breastbone) or the maxilla.

Buccal: Pertaining to the cheek; sometimes used to refer to the outer surface of a posterior tooth.

Calcification: The hardening of organic tissue because of deposits of calcium salts within the tissue.

Calculus: Calcified material adhering to the tooth surface either above the gingiva (supragingival calculus) or below the gingiva (subgingival calculus).

Capillary: Any of the minute, hair-like vessels connecting arteries and veins.

Cardiopulmonary Resuscitation (CPR): The combination of external cardiac compressions with artificial ventilation to revive a victim of cardiac arrest.

Caries: Decay of tooth structure.

Carpule: Trademark for a glass cartridge containing anesthetic solution, which is loaded into a syringe.

Cellulitis: Inflammation of cellular tissue.

Cementum: A bone-like substance that covers the tooth root and assists in supporting the tooth.

Cervical Line: A slight indentation that encircles a tooth, marking the junction of the crown with the root.

Chronic: Persisting over a long period of time; not acute.

Cingulum: A lingual elevation or lobe located within the cervical third of an anterior tooth.

Coagulation: The process by which blood changes from a fluid into a clot.

Congenital: Existing at birth.

Connective Tissue: The binding and supporting tissue of the body, such as bone, cartilage, and ligaments.

Contagious: Capable of being transmitted by contact from one person to another.

Contamination: The introduction of impurities or disease-producing organisms.

Contraction: The shortening, as of a muscle, in response to a stimulus.

Convulsion: Violent, involuntary contraction of the voluntary muscles.

Crown: The top part of a tooth. The anatomic crown is the part of the tooth covered with enamel. The clinical crown is the part of the tooth that is exposed (visible) in the mouth.

Cusp: A round or conical point on or near the working surface of a cuspid, bicuspid, or molar.

Cyanosis: Blueness of the skin, especially the area around the mouth and under the fingernails, due to lack of oxygen in the blood.

Cyst: A sac that contains liquid or semisolid material; usually an abnormal process.

Debridement: Surgical removal of foreign matter and damaged or infected tissue from a wound.

Deciduous: Not permanent; used to designate the teeth of the first dentition (the "baby teeth").

Dental Health Team: A team of two or more members—the dental officer, the dental assistant, and others—whose purpose is to serve the military community by caring for its dental health needs.

Dentin: That substance making up the bulk of the tooth. Primary dentin is formed before the tooth erupts; secondary dentin is formed after tooth eruption to protect the pulp from irritation.

Dentinoenamel Junction: The point at which the dentin and enamel meet.

Dentition: The natural teeth.

Diagnosis: The art of determining the nature of a disease.

Disease: Any departure from a state of health.

Disinfectant: An agent that destroys disease-producing microorganisms.

Distal: Away from the midline; the surface of a tooth that, following the curvature of the dental arch, faces away from the midline.

Edema: Swelling due to the collection of fluid in tissues.

Enamel: The hardest tissue of the body; it covers and protects the coronal portion of the dentin.

Enamel Hyoplasia: Defective or incomplete development of enamel.

Epiglottis: The lid-like structure that covers the entrance to the larynx.

Epithelial Attachment: The attachment of the gingiva to the tooth by means of epithelium.

Erosion: Wearing away or loss of tooth structure, usually resulting in smooth, shallow, V-like depressions.

Exudate: Fluid, cells, or cellular debris present in tissues or on tissue surfaces, usually as a result of inflammation or trauma.

Facial: Pertaining to the face; the outer (buccal and labial) surfaces of the teeth.

Fissure: A cleft or groove in the enamel on the occlusal surface of a tooth resulting from the imperfect union of cusp margins.

Foramen: A hole in a bone of the body that permits the passage of nerves and blood vessels.

Fossa: A shallow depression in the surface of a tooth.

Germicide: An agent that destroys bacteria.

Gingiva: The soft tissue covering the alveolar processes and encircling the necks of the teeth.

Gingivitis: Inflammation of the gingival tissue.

Groove: A linear depression in the surface of a tooth.

Hemorrhage: Bleeding.

Hemostat: An instrument or drug used to stop bleeding.

Horizontal Overlap: A condition in which the horizontal distance between the maxillary and mandibular incisal edges is abnormal when the other teeth are in normal occlusion. Also called overjet or "buck teeth."

Incisal Edge: The cutting edge of an anterior tooth.

Infection: Invasion of the tissues of the body by microorganisms in such a way as to favor their growth and development and permit their toxins to injure the tissues.

Inflammation: The reaction of tissue to irritation or injury, usually characterized by pain, heat, redness, and swelling.

Inlay: A restoration made outside the mouth and cemented into a prepared cavity.

Interproximal Space: The space between contacting (adjoining) teeth gingival to the contact area.

Labial: Pertaining to the lip; the outer (facial) surface of an anterior tooth.

Lateral: Toward the side or away from the midline.

Lesion: A change in structure or function of a tissue or part of the body due to injury or disease.

Line Angle: A line or angle formed by the junction of two surfaces of a tooth.

Lingual: Pertaining to the tongue; the surface of an anterior or posterior tooth that is toward the tongue.

Malocclusion: Any deviation from normal occlusion.

Mandible: The bone that forms the lower jaw.

Margin: The edge formed by joining together two surfaces, such as the distal and occlusal surfaces of posterior teeth.

Mastication: Chewing.

Maxillae: The two facial bones that unite to form the upper jaw.

Medial: Pertaining to the middle.

Median: Situated in the middle.

Membrane: A thin layer of tissue.

Mesial: Toward the midline; the surface of a tooth that, following the curvature of the dental arch, faces toward the midline.

Microorganism: A microscopically small living organism.

Mucosa: A mucous membrane, such as the lining of the oral cavity.

Necrosis: Death of a cell, or of a group of cells, in contact with living tissue.

Necrotic: Pertaining to or affected with necrosis.

Necrotizing Ulcerative Gingivitis (NUG): Severe inflammation of the gingival tissue.

Oblique Ridge: A ridge on the occlusal surface of a maxillary molar.

Occlusal: Pertaining to the chewing surfaces of posterior teeth.

Occlusion: The relationship between the occlusal surfaces of opposing maxillary and mandibular teeth when the teeth are in contact.

Odontoblast: Dentin-forming cell.

Osseous: Bony.

Palatal: Referring to the palate or roof of the mouth.

Palate: The roof of the mouth.

Papilla: Gingival tissue filling the interproximal space.

Pericoronitis: An inflammation of the gingiva around the crown of a partially erupted tooth.

Periodontal Abscess: An abscess caused by infection in the periodontium.

Periodontal Disease: A broad term for a number of diseases that affect the periodontium.

Periodontal Ligament: Fibrous tissue that surrounds a tooth root and attaches the root to its bony socket.

Periodontal Pocket: A gingival sulcus that has increased in depth because of periodontal disease.

Periodontitis: Inflammation of the periodontium.

Periodontium: The tissues that surround and support the teeth: the cementum, the alveolar process, the periodontal ligament, and the gingiva.

Pharmacology: The science dealing with the study of the action of drugs on living systems.

Point Angle: A point or angle formed by the junction of three surfaces of a tooth.

Posterior Teeth: Teeth located in the back of the mouth: the bicuspids and the molars.

Prescribe: To designate, recommend, or order a remedy or treatment.

Prescription: Written instructions for preparing and administering a remedy.

Pulp: The soft tissue that normally fills the pulp cavity. It contains nerve and blood vessels, maintains the vitality of the tooth, and forms dentin. Also referred to as the dental pulp.

Pus: A thick fluid formed in connection with inflammation.

Radiography: Recording images of a patient's internal structures on film by using X-rays.

Radiolucent: Permitting the passage of X-rays or other forms of radiation; refers to structures that appear dark on radiographs.

Radiopaque: Not permitting the passage of X-rays or other forms of radiation; refers to structures that appear light on radiographs.

Respiration: The act of breathing.

Restoration: The replacement of missing tooth structure; a material or device used for this purpose.

Resuscitation: The act of reviving a person who is unconscious or who appears to be dead.

Ridge: A linear elevation on a tooth.

Root Canal: Hollow, usually tubular, portion of the tooth root that extends from the pulp chamber to the apical foramen and serves as a passageway for nerves and blood vessels.

Sedative: An agent that allays apprehension, irritability, or excitement.

Shock: Acute circulatory failure due to inadequate volume of circulating blood, brought about by physical or emotional trauma.

Sterile: Free from living microorganisms.

Stomatitis: A general term used to denote inflammation of the oral mucosa.

Subcutaneous: Under the skin.

Supernumerary: Extra; more than the normal number.

Temporomandibular Joint (TMJ): The joint formed by the condyle of the mandible and the glenoid fossa of the temporal bone.

Therapy: Treatment.

Topical: Pertaining to the surface.

Trachea: The windpipe.

Tragus: A projection of cartilage located in front of the external opening of the ear.

Tranquilizer: An agent that induces calmness.

Transverse Ridge: A ridge on the occlusal surface of a tooth formed by the junction of the facial and lingual triangular ridges.

Trauma: Injury or wound.

Triangular Ridge: A ridge on the occlusal surface of a tooth that slopes down from the tip of a cusp toward the center of the occlusal surface.

Trituration: The process of mixing mercury with a metal alloy to produce a plastic mass suitable for use in restoring teeth.

Ulcer: An open sore on the skin or mucous membrane.

Unconscious: Insensible; unaware of self or environment.

Vertical Overlap: A condition in which the vertical distance between the maxillary and mandibular incisal edges is abnormal when the other teeth are in normal occlusion. Also called overbite.

Wisdom Tooth: A term used for the third molar.

www.ingramcontent.com/pod-product-compliance
Lightning Source LLC
Chambersburg PA
CBHW081827300426
44116CB00014B/2504